The Environment

Other Books of Related Interest:

Opposing Viewpoints Series

Eco-Architecture

Endangered Oceans

Natural Disasters

Nuclear Power

At Issue Series

Are Natural Disasters Increasing?

Can Glacier and Ice Melt Be Reversed?

Fracking

Hybrid and Electric Cars

Wind Farms

Current Controversies Series

Biodiversity

Factory Farming

Global Warming

Pesticides

Pollution

"Congress shall make
no law . . . abridging
the freedom of speech,
or of the press."

First Amendment to the US Constitution

The basic foundation of our democracy is the First Amendment guarantee of freedom of expression. The Opposing Viewpoints Series is dedicated to the concept of this basic freedom and the idea that it is more important to practice it than to enshrine it.

The Environment

Lynn M. Zott, Book Editor

GREENHAVEN PRESS
A part of Gale, Cengage Learning

GALE
CENGAGE Learning·

Farmington Hills, Mich • San Francisco • New York • Waterville, Maine
Meriden, Conn • Mason, Ohio • Chicago

Elizabeth Des Chenes, *Director, Content Strategy*
Douglas Dentino, *Manager, New Product*

For more information, contact:
Greenhaven Press
27500 Drake Rd.
Farmington Hills, MI 48331-3535
Or you can visit our Internet site at gale.cengage.com

LIBRARY OF CONGRESS CATALOGING-IN-PUBLICATION DATA

The environment / Lynn M. Zott, book editor.
       pages cm. -- (Opposing viewpoints)
    Summary: "Opposing Viewpoints: The Environment: Opposing Viewpoints is the leading source for libraries and classrooms in need of current-issue materials. The viewpoints are selected from a wide range of highly respected sources and publications" -- Provided by publisher.
    Includes bibliographical references and index.
    ISBN 978-0-7377-6654-7 (hardback) -- ISBN 978-0-7377-6655-4 (paperback)
    1. Environmental degradation. 2. Environmental degradation--United States. 3. Environmental quality--United States. 4. Environmental policy. 5. Environmental policy--United States. 6. Environmental protection. 7. Environmental protection--United States. I. Zott, Lynn M. (Lynn Marie), 1969-, editor of compilation.
    GE140.E5333 2014
    363.7--dc23
                                                                2014003360

Printed in the United States of America
1 2 3 4 5 6 7 18 17 16 15 14

Contents

Chapter 3: Are Western Societies' Practices Bad for the Environment?

Chapter 4: What Policies Will Improve the Environment?

Why Consider
Opposing Viewpoints?

"The only way in which a human being can make some approach to knowing the whole of a subject is by hearing what can be said about it by persons of every variety of opinion and studying all modes in which it can be looked at by every character of mind. No wise man ever acquired his wisdom in any mode but this."

John Stuart Mill

In our media-intensive culture it is not difficult to find differing opinions. Thousands of newspapers and magazines and dozens of radio and television talk shows resound with differing points of view. The difficulty lies in deciding which opinion to agree with and which "experts" seem the most credible. The more inundated we become with differing opinions and claims, the more essential it is to hone critical reading and thinking skills to evaluate these ideas. Opposing Viewpoints books address this problem directly by presenting stimulating debates that can be used to enhance and teach these skills. The varied opinions contained in each book examine many different aspects of a single issue. While examining these conveniently edited opposing views, readers can develop critical thinking skills such as the ability to compare and contrast authors' credibility, facts, argumentation styles, use of persuasive techniques, and other stylistic tools. In short, the Opposing Viewpoints Series is an ideal way to attain the higher-level thinking and reading skills so essential in a culture of diverse and contradictory opinions.

In addition to providing a tool for critical thinking, Opposing Viewpoints books challenge readers to question their own strongly held opinions and assumptions. Most people form their opinions on the basis of upbringing, peer pressure, and personal, cultural, or professional bias. By reading carefully balanced opposing views, readers must directly confront new ideas as well as the opinions of those with whom they disagree. This is not to argue simplistically that everyone who reads opposing views will—or should—change his or her opinion. Instead, the series enhances readers' understanding of their own views by encouraging confrontation with opposing ideas. Careful examination of others' views can lead to the readers' understanding of the logical inconsistencies in their own opinions, perspective on why they hold an opinion, and the consideration of the possibility that their opinion requires further evaluation.

Evaluating Other Opinions

To ensure that this type of examination occurs, Opposing Viewpoints books present all types of opinions. Prominent spokespeople on different sides of each issue as well as well-known professionals from many disciplines challenge the reader. An additional goal of the series is to provide a forum for other, less known, or even unpopular viewpoints. The opinion of an ordinary person who has had to make the decision to cut off life support from a terminally ill relative, for example, may be just as valuable and provide just as much insight as a medical ethicist's professional opinion. The editors have two additional purposes in including these less known views. One, the editors encourage readers to respect others' opinions—even when not enhanced by professional credibility. It is only by reading or listening to and objectively evaluating others' ideas that one can determine whether they are worthy of consideration. Two, the inclusion of such viewpoints encourages the important critical thinking skill of objectively evaluating an author's credentials and bias. This evaluation will illuminate an author's reasons for taking a particular stance on an issue and will aid in readers' evaluation of the author's ideas.

It is our hope that these books will give readers a deeper understanding of the issues debated and an appreciation of the complexity of even seemingly simple issues when good and honest people disagree. This awareness is particularly important in a democratic society such as ours in which people enter into public debate to determine the common good. Those with whom one disagrees should not be regarded as enemies but rather as people whose views deserve careful examination and may shed light on one's own.

Thomas Jefferson once said that "difference of opinion leads to inquiry, and inquiry to truth." Jefferson, a broadly educated man, argued that "if a nation expects to be ignorant and free . . . it expects what never was and never will be." As individuals and as a nation, it is imperative that we consider the opinions of others and examine them with skill and discernment. The Opposing Viewpoints Series is intended to help readers achieve this goal.

David L. Bender and Bruno Leone,
Founders

Introduction

> *"We stand now where two roads diverge. But unlike the roads in Robert Frost's familiar poem, they are not equally fair. The road we have long been traveling is deceptively easy, a smooth superhighway on which we progress with great speed, but at its end lies disaster. The other fork of the road—the one less traveled by—offers our last, our only, chance to reach a destination that assures the preservation of the earth."*
>
> —Rachel Carson,
> Silent Spring, *1962*

Typhoon Haiyan, one of the most severe category five hurricanes ever recorded, made landfall in the Philippines on November 9, 2013, more than a week after the hurricane season officially ended on November 1. Because the storm reached its peak size and strength—an estimated three hundred miles across, wave surges thirteen feet high, and estimated wind speeds upwards of 190 miles per hour—just as it also reached land, its effects were devastating. As of December 4, 2013, the death toll from Haiyan was at 5,719, with 1,779 people still missing. The economic damage resulting from Haiyan, was "$390 billion in damaged infrastructure and the same amount again in ruined crops."[1]

Many scientists contend that so-called supertyphoons and other types of superstorms will become more frequent and even commonplace as the oceans warm and give more energy and intensity to tropical storms. They indicate that although the overall frequency of storms will not increase, the incidence of severe storms, rated category four or five (on a scale of one to five), will continue to climb as the planet warms. The connection between extreme weather and climate change was a frequent subject of debate in 2012, when Hurricane Sandy (aka Superstorm Sandy) wreaked havoc on the United States' Eastern Seaboard. Meteorologist Jeff Masters reported on his blog that Hurricane Sandy

> was the most powerful and second most destructive Atlantic hurricane in recorded history. Ten hours before landfall, at 9:30 am EDT October 29, the total energy of Sandy's winds of tropical storm–force and higher peaked at 329 tera-joules—the highest value for any Atlantic hurricane since at least 1969, and equivalent to more than five Hiroshima-sized atomic bombs. At landfall, Sandy's tropical storm–force winds spanned 943 miles of the U.S. coast. No hurricane on record has been larger. . . . Sandy's late-season show of unprecedented strength, unusual track, and exceptionally damaging storm surge were made more likely due to climate change, and the storm helped bring more awareness and debate about the threat of climate change to the U.S. than any event since Hurricane Katrina in 2005.[2]

Record-setting heat plagued much of the United States in 2012, breaking twenty-six thousand high-temperature records that year alone. The extensive drought conditions that plagued up to 63 percent of the United States in 2012 led to wildfires across 9,101,461 acres of the land, with the worst fires in Colorado, Oregon, and Washington. Not only were the fires intense and widespread, but they occurred much earlier in the season than expected. Kevin Trenberth, a senior scientist for the National Center for Atmospheric Research, indicated in a July 2, 2012, interview on PBS's *NewsHour* that

> now we're going outside of the realm of conditions previously experienced. And so that's when the damage really becomes extreme, and we get all of these wildfires. Houses have been burned, tremendous damage to the environment and, you know, maybe some other consequences to come

with regard to things like bugs that have survived the relatively warm winter. So these are all manifestations of climate change that we expect to see more of as time goes on. . . . With an unchanging climate, you expect that the number of highs and the number of low temperature records are about the same. And that was the case in the 1950s, '60s and '70s. And then by the 2000s, we were breaking high temperature records at a ratio of 2-to-1 over cold temperature records. But this year, we have been breaking high-temperature records at a rate of about 10-to-1. . . . So, breaking records is not an indication of climate change. But breaking records at a rate of 10-to-1 vs. the cold records, that's a clear indication of climate change.[3]

While some cautioned against or directly refuted the notion that 2012's extreme weather was influenced by climate change, a report published in the September 2013 issue of the *Bulletin of the American Meteorological Society* supports this claim. The study, which examined twelve extreme weather events from 2012, including Hurricane Sandy, record temperatures, and widespread drought, and incorporated research from nineteen different scientific teams worldwide, concluded that "approximately half of the analyses found some evidence that anthropogenic [human-made] climate change was a contributing factor to the extreme event examined, though the effects of natural fluctuations of weather and climate on the evolution of many of the extreme events played key roles as well."[4] In a letter published in the August 2013 issue of *Nature*, the authors indicate that a decrease in the variability of weather is a greater source of concern than overall warming in relation to extreme weather, and they maintain that "greater emphasis now needs to be placed on analysing changes in climate variability in the context of anthropogenic climate change, so as to inform more effective adaptation strategies."[5] In an editorial in the *Washington Post*, Danish environmentalist and university professor Bjørn Lomborg uses the *Nature* letter's authors' statement that "our findings contradict the view that a warming world will automatically be one of more overall climatic variation" to bolster his contention that "the argument that global warming generally creates more extreme weather needs to be retired."[6]

The controversy over climate change's relationship to extreme weather is only one of the many facets of the current debate over environmental issues covered in *Opposing Viewpoints: The Environment*. In chapters titled "Is There a Global Environmental Crisis?," "How Should Climate Change Be Addressed?," "Are Western Societies' Practices Bad for the Environment?," and "What Policies Will Improve the Environment?," viewpoint authors discuss the existence and source of climate change, the scope of climate change and other environmental threats, the most appropriate and effective responses to various environmental issues, the impact of Western societies' lifestyles and business practices, and what policies represent the best opportunities for curbing damage to the environment and addressing and reducing existing environmental threats.

Notes

1. Per Liljas, "Supertyphoon Haiyan: Death Toll Reaches 5,719," *Time*, December 4, 2013. http://world.time.com.

2. Jeff Masters, "Top Ten Global Weather Events of 2012," *Weather Underground Blog*, January 11, 2013. www.wunderground.com.

3. Kevin Trenberth with Judy Woodruff, "What's Causing Unusually Hot Temperatures in U.S.?," *NewsHour*, PBS, July 2, 2012. www.pbs.org.

4. Thomas C. Peterson, Martin P. Hoerling, Peter A. Stott, and Stephanie C. Herring, eds. "Explaining Extreme Events of 2012 from a Climate Perspective," *Bulletin of the American Meteorological Society*, Special Supplement, September 2013, p. 80.

5. Chris Huntingford, Philip D. Jones, Valerie N. Livina, Timothy M. Lenton, and Peter M. Cox, "No Increase in Global Temperature Variability Despite Changing Regional Patterns," *Nature*, August 15, 2013. www.nature.com.

6. Bjørn Lomborg, "Don't Blame Climate Change for Extreme Weather," *Washington Post*, September 13, 2013. http://articles.washingtonpost.com.

CHAPTER 1

Is There a Global Environmental Crisis?

Chapter Preface

Ear wax samples taken from a dead whale tell a story of chemical pollution in the Pacific Ocean. Similar to the rings found inside felled trees, the layers of wax taken from a whale's ear canal provide a history of the whale's environment throughout its life. Researchers extracted a ten-inch long ear-wax column from a seventy-foot blue whale killed in a collision with a ship off the coast of Santa Barbara, California, in 2007. According to Amina Khan in a September 2013 article in the *Los Angeles Times*, "The chemical contaminants found—from flame retardants, pesticides and other pollutants . . . opened a porthole onto humans' long-term effects on the ocean." In addition to several other pollutants, the researchers found DDT, an insecticide that was banned in the United States in 1972 because it was suspected of causing cancer. The DDT discovery was alarming, since the twelve-year-old whale had been born long after the DDT ban was put in place. "In fact, a full 96% of the total burden of organic pollutants in its wax came from four historic-use pesticides (and their metabolites) and a PCB [polychlorinated biphenyl], a type of chemical used in coolants and insulating fluids," Khan reports. Researchers explained that many of the chemicals found were likely passed to the whale through its mother's milk during the first six months of its life. These researchers have asked other scientists around the world to collect similar samples to compare the data found worldwide.

In their introductory editorial for a September 2013 special issue of the *Marine Pollution Bulletin*, Alex D. Rogers and Dan Laffoley caution that climate change, pollution, and humans' overuse of marine resources through fishing and shipping are, especially in combination, rapidly changing and in many cases destroying marine ecosystems around the world. Human-created carbon dioxide emissions are particularly worrisome, Rogers and Laffoley contend, because CO_2 alters the function and nature of marine ecosystems in a manner that speeds up global warming. They conclude: "The continued expansion in global population exerts ever increasing pressures on scarcer ocean resources through overexploitation and on marine ecosystems through indirect impacts such as pollution. It is therefore important to recognise that growing impacts on the ocean are inseparable from the population growth and per-capita resource use, and tackling these issues underlies the reduction of the footprint of humankind on all ecosystems. Human interactions with the ocean must change with the rapid adoption of a holistic approach to sustainable management of all activities that impinge on marine ecosystems."

Pollution in the world's oceans and human-caused damage to the marine ecosystem is one area of a global environmental threat that many believe has reached the point of crisis. Authors of viewpoints in the following chapter debate other global environmental issues, including climate change (or global warming) and freshwater shortage, and their relative threat to the planet and its inhabitants.

> "*The rate of species extinction is now 1,000 times as great as it was before the coming of humanity.*"

There Are Multiple Threats to the Earth's Environment

Brian Parham

Brian Parham is a contributor to The Bridge, *an online publication for Portland Community College. In the following viewpoint, Parham interviews Tim Vendlinski who outlines the five major threats to the earth's environment—biogenetic diversity loss, deforestation, climate change, unstable energy policy and overreliance on fossil fuels, and water and soil resource depletion—as well as the related issues stemming from these five. Vendlinski discusses the human contribution to these threats and the consequences of such actions. Further, this viewpoint delves into the natural losses caused by human interaction and the increasing extinction rates if these threats continue.*

As you read, consider the following questions:

1. According to the author, at what rate are the rainforests being cleared each year?

2. What country does the author cite as being number one in terms of carbon dioxide emissions?

3. According to Vendlinski, all life relies on what around the planet?

Mass extinction. Arctic sea melts. Collapsing world fisheries. Raging fires. Crippling droughts and modern dust bowls.

The environment—and our ability to survive on it—is being pushed to the brink.

I interviewed long-time environmental professional, scientist, and community activist Tim Vendlinski, to discuss the five gravest issues facing the environment today and—more importantly—what each of us can do to help to save the planet.

Tim Vendlinski began his career as an environmental advocate when he was 10 years old. "In the elementary school I attended there was this big oak forest behind us. Then one day, all these bulldozers showed up and started tearing the oak trees down," Vendlinski said. "Well, to the horror of the school principal and teachers, I led a band of students to the construction site and stopped them from cutting the trees down."

Vendlinski later earned his associate's degree from the American River College, saved Arcade Creek—the last intact watershed—forest in Sacramento as a teenager, and completed his bachelor's degree in environmental policy and planning from the University of California.

Now at age 53, Tim has been fighting for the environment for over 40 years.

The Loss of Biogenetic Diversity

The earth is now experiencing one of the greatest mass extinction in the planet's history. The rate of species extinction is now 1,000 times as great as it was before the coming of humanity.

"This is the biggest ecological disaster—in terms of sheer extinction," Vendlinski said. "We have lost more plants and animals today than when the dinosaurs died out 65 million years ago."

Although extinction is a natural process, human activities like deforestation accelerate these natural processes. In the past, an individual species disappeared naturally at a rate of about one species per year and was replaced by a new species. Scientists are now calling this environmental disaster the "modern extinction crisis."

If current extinction rates continue, one half of all species on earth will be extinct in 100 years. "It's a philosophical and spiritual problem. We should be protecting life. Life has an intrinsic value. We should honor life," Vendlinski said. "But practically speaking, many, if not most, of the pharmaceutical chemicals on the market were derived from natural sources."

Deforestation

At the heart of these modern environmental disasters lie corruption, greed, and economics. Lumber, petroleum, and mining companies build roads into the jungles. Governments encourage the poor people to settle in these regions, who must clear it for farming. Cattle ranchers require vast expanses for their herds, and land speculators clear huge areas for expected profits.

However, the recovered land is fragile, creating a cycle of further destruction.

This process is known as deforestation.

Tropical rainforests cover about 7 percent of the earth's dry land. But those rainforests are being cleared at a rate of about 8.5 million hectares per year. "When you look at the rate of the Amazon deforestation each year, it's 100s if not 1000s of square miles each year," Vendlinski said.

According to the National Geographic's website, "Deforestation has many negative effects on the environment. The most dramatic impact is a loss of habitat for millions of species. Seventy percent of Earth's land animals and plants live in forests, and many cannot survive the deforestation that destroys their homes."

Deforestation is also responsible for regulating water cycles, absorbing greenhouse gases, and stabilizing the earth's climate.

Climate Change

The earth is warming. The arctic ice is melting, glaciers are shrinking, and sea levels are rising.

In 2007, the Intergovernmental Panel on Climate Change, an international coalition of the world's top scientists, declared climate change real and man made. According to their data, IPCC concluded the warming of the climate system is "unequivocal."

"The year 2012 was the hottest year ever recorded in the United States," Vendlinski said. "In fact, the 10 warmest years on record occured during the last 15 years."[1]

These increased temperatures are also causing more extreme weather across the country.

"We have accelerated temperature increases with human activities, and we make the weather more extreme," Vendlinski said. "So events like droughts, record highs, or hurricanes are now more extreme."

Climate change is now creating an unstable world and affecting global food production.

Unsustainable Energy Policy and Overreliance on Fossil Fuels

During the Industrial Revolution, human beings harnessed the power of fossil fuels—coal, oil, and natural gas. For the first time in history, machines replaced man and animal power. Global populations skyrocketed. Economies flourished. And empires were born.

---

1. See www.nytimes.com/2013/01/09/science/earth/2012-was-hottest-year-ever-in -us.html?_r=0.

But progress came at a heavy price.

First, fossil fuels are a non-renewable energy source. They take millions of years to develop, and they are being depleted much faster than they are being formed. And second, the burning of fossil fuels produces approximately 21.3 billion tons of carbon dioxide (CO_2) per year.

This is where the lines begin to blur. Fossil fuels, deforestation, and global warming are so closely related, it's hard to see where one issue ends and the other begins. Like the glaciers, the distinctions melt away.

After all, carbon dioxide—caused by the burning of fossil fuels—is the prime contributor to global warming.

And when it comes to carbon dioxide emissions today, the United States is public enemy number two, behind China. Indeed, the U.S. economy is built on fossil fuels. In fact, we consume more oil and natural gas than any other country, and we rank second—behind China—in coal consumption.

"When Vice President Dick Cheney was in office, the Bush Administration energy policy was crafted by oil companies," Vendlinski said. "The administration formulated their energy policies just with the energy companies."

Although the United States has 4.5 percent of the world's population, it produced 18 percent of the world's carbon dioxide emissions in 2010, according to the U.S. Energy Information Administration.

For years, scientists and climate experts around the world have warned us 350 parts per million was the upper threshold of CO_2 in the atmosphere. Once beyond 350 ppm, they cautioned global warming could spin out of control.

Today, the planet has 392 parts per million CO_2. According to 350.org, we need to act fast if we want a livable planet.

"While the Bush Administration was belittling scientists and environmentalists on climate change," Vendlinski said, "they were simultaneously preparing to take advantage of the melting ice sheet to exploit the oil resources."

Our voracious appetite for fossil fuels has many other consequences including: polluting local environments by drilling for oil, leaking pipelines, discharging underground tanks, spilling oil from shipping accidents, the routine flushing of tanks, and deep-sea drilling accidents.

Depletion of Water and Soil Resources

Across the planet, a thin, three-foot layer of topsoil provides food crops for 6.8 billion people and grazing for about 4 billion domesticated animals, but this nutrient-rich topsoil is in jeopardy.

"All life relies on the first few feet of soil around the planet," Vendlinski said. "We have the atmosphere, and we have those first few feet of soil."

Scientists now estimate that we are losing roughly one percent of our topsoil every year because of careless husbandry, urbanization, plowing, overuse, irrigation, and chemical fertilizers.

"In addition, we are destroying our fresh water supplies around the world," Vendlinski said. "Through direct pollution, mismanagement of our rivers, and the depletion and poisoning of our groundwater."

Our rivers, lakes and oceans are being polluted by industrial waste, farm byproducts (such as herbicides, fertilizers, and animal waste), city sewage, and oil spills.

Today, contaminated water kills more than 5 million people worldwide and nearly 1.2 billion people do not have access to safe drinking water.

Like the rest of these issues, the distinction between land and water issues evaporates upon inspection.

"Rivers are expressions of their terrestrial surroundings," Vendlinski said, "The rivers are there because of everything around it. The trees. The forests. The way the water moves off the land."

In addition, fish populations are on the verge of extinction, the oceans are becoming more acidic, and coral reefs are disappearing.

> *"For the first time since these [IPCC] reports started coming out in 1990, the new one dials back the alarm."*

New Report Undercuts Global Warming Alarmists

Michael Barone

Michael Barone is a contributing writer for the Washington Examiner. *In the following viewpoint, Barone likens the belief that global warming is both real and a cause for alarm to religion, because, he says, this belief is based on faith rather than on observable reality. Like the mid-nineteenth-century religious sect the Millerites, Barone contends, global warming alarmists are facing a devastating challenge to their faith. For the Millerites, he explains, this challenge occurred when Jesus failed to return to earth on the prophesied date. Global warming alarmists, he argues, are shaken by the evidence revealed in the fifth assessment report of the International Panel on Climate Change (IPCC) indicating that global temperatures have not risen to the extent predicted by scientific models and have not increased during the last fifteen years. Barone draws parallels between practices of religious followers and those of global warming alarmists, and asserts that the alarmists seek to impose their beliefs on oth-*

ers. Barone maintains that global warming alarmists' carbon emissions reduction policies have been widely rejected and that their proposed and implemented alternative sources of energy production have been an abject failure.

As you read, consider the following questions:

1. What was the date the Millerites believed Jesus would return to earth, according to Barone?

2. To whom do some global warming alarmists compare "denialists," according to the author?

3. What church does Barone say was formed by some former Millerites?

Events have failed to fulfill the prophecy. Preachers have suddenly been struck dumb by uncertainty. Believers are understandably nervous and some, under their breath, are abandoning the dogma.

These sentences could have been written at the end of the day on Oct. 22, 1844, about the Millerites, a religious sect started in upstate New York. Preachers had told their followers that Jesus would return to earth that day. He failed to show.

But the subject here is not Millerism but another kind of religious faith: the faith of the global warming alarmists. And while it's not likely to have the impact of the Millerites' Great Disappointment, we could be seeing the beginning of something similar on September 27 [2013] when the Intergovernmental Panel on Climate Change issues its fifth assessment report in Stockholm.

Real Change vs. Predicted Change

A preview is provided by science writer Matt Ridley in *The Wall Street Journal*, who has "had a glimpse of the key prediction at the heart of the document."

"The big news," Ridley writes, "is that, for the first time since these reports started coming out in 1990, the new one dials back the alarm. It states that the temperature rise we can expect as a result of man-made emissions of carbon dioxide is lower than the IPCC thought in 2007."

Ridley admits that the change is small. And he does not deny that increased carbon emissions could increase global temperatures by some significant amount. They would certainly do so if carbon emissions were the only thing affecting climate.

But there may be other things. Like variations in sun activity. "The most plausible explanation of the pause," Ridley writes, "is simply that climate sensitivity was overestimated in the models because of faulty assumptions about net amplification through water-vapor feedback."

The pause referred to is the fact that global temperatures haven't increased over the last 15 years. Global warming models predicted they would. The models' failure is not as stark as the Great Disappointment. But it's a failure nonetheless.

Global Warming Alarmism as Religion

The religious analogy is appropriate because belief in global warming has taken on the trappings of traditional religion.

Alarmists like to say the science is settled—which is nonsense, since science is a series of theories that can be tested by observations. When [Albert] Einstein presented his theory of relativity he showed how it could be tested during astronomical events in the next decade. The theory passed.

Saying the science is settled is demanding what religions demand, that you have faith.

Religion has ritual. Global warming alarmism has recycling and Earth Day celebrations.

Some religions persecute heretics. Some global warming alarmists identify "denialists" and liken them to [the Nazi] Holocaust deniers.

Humans Have Not Caused Global Warming

Yeah, the sea level has been rising. Exactly the same as it has been for thousands of years, since the end of the last actual Ice Age. It has nothing to do with my SUV.

Moreover, the pattern of global temperature change has not followed rising atmospheric CO_2 since the advent of the Industrial Revolution. It follows instead the up and down patterns of ocean churning temperature cycles and of solar activity, such as sun spots that were so influential in causing the Little Ice Age that ended roughly a couple of hundred years ago. . . . Natural causes, not human factors like CO_2 emissions, have predominated in causing climate change.

Peter Ferrara,
Forbes, September 22, 2013.

Religions build grand places of worship. Global warming alarmists promote the construction of windmills and solar farms that produce uneconomic and intermittent electricity.

Global warming alarmism even has indulgences like the ones [German Protestant Reformation leader] Martin Luther protested. You can buy carbon offsets to gain forgiveness for travel on carbon-emitting private jet aircraft.

Some religions ban vulgar pleasures, like the New England Puritan sumptuary laws banning luxuries. Some global warming alarmists want to force most Americans out of big-lawn suburbs into high-rise apartments clustered around mass transit stations.

This last element seems to be dominant among many global warming alarmists. Stop the vulgar masses from living their tacky lifestyles driving those horrid SUVs. They must be made to repent, conform and be saved.

Carbon Emissions Reductions Have Failed

The signs that the threat of global warming has been exaggerated come after alarmists' demands for vast carbon emission reductions have been rejected by publics here and abroad.

The European Union's carbon reduction program is in a shambles and the United States has actually reduced emissions more, thanks to cheap natural gas produced by fracking.

Windmills and solar panels are not economical or dependable sources of electricity. China and India are not going to stifle the economic growth that is lifting millions out of poverty with carbon emission caps.

History teaches that climate can change, and it makes sense to fund research to determine how to mitigate possible harms (and capitalize on possible benefits).

Unfortunately, most government and nonprofit funding has gone to global warming alarmists. But apparently even these priests understand that their prophecies have not been fulfilled.

Redemption is possible. Some Millerites formed the Seventh Day Adventist church, which has built fine medical schools and hospitals. Global warming alarmists might consider their example.

| "Groundwater depletion is a global phenomenon."

The Earth's Water Supply Is in Grave Danger

Jay Famiglietti

Jay Famiglietti is a hydrologist and a professor of earth system science in the School of Physical Sciences, a professor of civil and environmental engineering in the Henry Samueli School of Engineering, and the director of the Center for Hydrologic Modeling, all at the University of California, Irvine. In the following viewpoint, Famiglietti argues that while there is no possibility of ending the global water crisis, there are ways in which humanity can better manage its freshwater supply to make it cleaner and more widely available. In addition to the dual challenges of poor water quality and low availability, he says the global water crisis involves a lack of clear leadership, economic resources, and understanding about the true extent and nature of the crisis. In order to accomplish everything that needs to happen to address the water crisis, he concludes, strong public and private leadership and partnerships must emerge to drive US and international water policy in the right direction. Environmentally friendly and sustainable policies, Famiglietti asserts, would benefit both the water supply and the economy.

As you read, consider the following questions:

1. What does Famiglietti say that he and others have used to track changes in freshwater availability?

2. According to the author, at least how many people rely on groundwater as their primary water source?

3. What does Famiglietti say that people need to keep them from sticking their heads in the sand after hearing so much bad news?

Last month [May 2013] I had an opportunity to give a TEDx talk on my home campus at UC [University of California] Irvine. Mine was called "Can We End the Global Water Crisis?" I'd like to share my views on this topic with our [National Geographic's] Water Currents readers by posting several excerpts, more or less straight from the talk.

"Can we end the global water crisis? . . . No, we can't end it. I'm sorry. It's too big for humanity to beat down and conquer. We've passed too many tipping points—with climate change and with population growth and with human behavior—to be able to turn an extremely critical situation around."

So, why bother taking action? Because we still can make a difference!

"I truly believe that with a shared vision, with leadership and commitment from governments around the world, and with public and private partnerships, we can *manage* our way through to ensure a *sustainable* water future."

I thought it would be a good idea to define the global water crisis in the context of my talk. Here's what I put forward:

"In it's simplest form, the global water crisis is the inability to provide a reliable supply of potable water to villages, towns, cities and regional populations, all over the world. Globally, about a billion people around the world lack *reliable* access to *potable* water.

"When I think about the global water crisis I see several key components. . . .

"There are the obvious crises of freshwater *availability* and of water *quality*—is there enough water available in a particular region, and is it clean enough so that when we drink it we don't get sick?

The Water Crisis Is Multilayered

"However, even where water is available and clean, we see:

"A *crisis of management:* are water resources being managed efficiently, or, is there a government commitment to even deliver water to its people?

"A *crisis of economics:* does a country have the wealth to build and maintain the infrastructure to treat and distribute water?

"And a *crisis of understanding:* does the public and do our elected officials really understand what's happening with water, nationally and globally? If they did, I contend that we could make some real progress towards managing this crisis."

I made the point that hydrologists like myself have a clear mission "*to help elevate awareness of critical water issues to the level of everyday understanding.*"

Much of my talk focused on our research using the NASA GRACE satellite mission to track how freshwater availability is changing around the world. Some of that work has been written about in Water Currents before; for example, our work in India, California and the Middle East have all been highlighted. Most recently we've published a map of the United States that shows several regional hotspots where groundwater depletion is threatening water supply reserves, or where increasingly wet conditions are leading to regional flooding.

However, my bottom line was this:

"Now we can see that groundwater depletion is a global phenomenon. At least 2 billion people rely on groundwater as their primary water source, and most of their water comes from these aquifers that are at risk of running dry in the coming decades. . ." so that the number of people who currently already lack access to a reliable supply of potable freshwater (∼1 billion) is on the rise.

I'm no expert in water quality, but I do know this:

"The history of humanity, and of economic development, has had at least a couple of distinct phases with respect to water quality—an early phase in which we really didn't understand how the water cycle worked so we did things like dump toxic materials right on the ground or directly into rivers; and a more recent phase in which we actually know better, but choose to do it anyway, because it's easy and cheap.

Work Is Needed, Yet Hope Exists

"The unfortunate reality is that we humans have been living along or above our water supplies for a very, very long time, doing our thing for century after century, all the while using our waters as an all too convenient dumping grounds. It should come as no surprise—but yet it does for many people—that most of our waters around the world, where we still have them, are dangerously dirty and require considerable and expensive treatment before we can use them."

One thing I've learned over the years is that in order to keep people from sticking their heads in the sand after hearing all of this bad news, is that they need hope. They need to feel empowered. They need to know that there is a pathway forward, and that if we work together, we can *definitely* make a difference.

I returned to some of my favorite themes, which I will probably keep writing and talking about until a) we actually start doing something about it; or b) I die. I anticipate that both will take a while, but you never know.

"First, we need to figure out how much freshwater we actually *have* on the planet. The truth is that we really don't

Facts About World Water Consumption

85% of the world population lives in the driest half of the planet.

783 million people do not have access to clean water and almost 2.5 billion do not have access to adequate sanitation. . . .

Water for irrigation and food production constitutes one of the greatest pressures on freshwater resources. Agriculture accounts for ~70% of global freshwater withdrawals (up to 90% in some fast-growing economies).

United Nations, World Water Day 2013. www.unwater.org.

know. Especially groundwater. It's our biggest stock of freshwater, yet we have not done the exploration that we need to, and that's just unacceptable.

"Second, we need to determine how much water we actually *need*, to grow food, for industry, to generate power and for domestic use. And by all means, let's not forget the environment. Humans cannot expect to use all available waters and still have a healthy planet to live on.

"Third, how are both of these, and the gaps between them, *changing* over time, with climate change, with population growth, and with increased awareness, conservation and efficiency."

Feeling feisty, I threw down the virtual gauntlet:

"Today I challenge our government and others around the world to do the exploration that needs doing. If water is in fact the new oil, let's finally do the exploration with the same vigor. We cannot begin to address sustainability issues unless we actually know how much water we have.

Improving Conservation and Efficiency

"Let's actually monitor groundwater withdrawals, both public and private. Right now, in many parts of the world, including most states in the U.S., if you own property, you can pump the groundwater beneath it at will, even if that means that you are drawing in water from beneath your neighbor's property. It's not unlike having several straws in a glass of water, and everyone sipping at will. If we want to make the water in the glass last, the free-for-all must end at once.

"Let's focus on improved water conservation and efficiency, especially in agriculture, the biggest use of water around the globe. We can do so much more with so much less. We need more efficient irrigation, better crop selection, more saline and drought tolerant crops, more greenhouse agriculture, and yes, better pricing. Here we need to look to world leaders in conservation and efficiency like Israel.

"Only after we've done these easier and cheaper things should we significantly ramp up our recycling and desalination efforts. But don't get me wrong—these are already both critical components of water security in many regions around the world, including right here in Southern California."

And now, a pitch for public-private partnerships. I feel strongly about what I said next, and as above, you will continue to hear this from me into the foreseeable future.

"The realities of our modern economy are that there are many demands for a limited amount of funds. This is where vision and leadership come into play. We need champions in our state and local governments to carry the torch.

Wanted: Vision and Leadership

"And beyond governments, we need more public and private partnerships to move this agenda forward. The private sector has the resources and the agility to partner with our universities and research labs to make a huge impact. Many of the technologies that we need to monitor and manage water much more efficiently already exist. Public-private partnerships can make this happen far more quickly than convincing a giant bureaucracy."

Denouement time: we can't end the global water crisis, but. . .

"We can take steps to manage our way through this global crisis and ensure a sustainable water future for everyone. But we need to confront the realities that I've shared with you today, head on, and begin to deal with them now.

"Water availability *will* be more contentious in the future. We can see the haves and have nots developing already. However, water can also be a vehicle for peacebuiliding, since these transboundary, regional problems require transboundary, regional solutions.

"Therefore, we need to deal, now, with the required political and legal frameworks and the civil infrastructure to peaceably share, use and reuse water, within regions and across political boundaries.

"We need a national water policy in the U.S., and we need new, global, international water law.

"And we need to integrate water discussions into the fabric of our diplomatic efforts, especially in places like the Middle East and other hotspots where threats to water security may trigger violent conflict.

Green Policies Can Grow the Economy

"We can and must take back our environment, including our water environment. Economic growth and environmental preservation are not mutually exclusive. A green economy can be a very, very strong economy, and the water sector can be a big part of that. And remember, without water, we don't even have an economy.

"The nexus of water and energy and food will define our quality of life in this century. It already is.

"Ultimately, water will be limiting in all respects, unless we learn to do more with a lot less, and to reuse and reuse more and more, and to manage our way to a sustainable water future."

That's my message. A little dramatic for sure, but it was after all a TEDx talk, so I wanted to just hang it all out there. Thanks for reading. If I have inspired you, please, share this with your family, friends and colleagues. We need your help to spread the word.

VIEWPOINT

| *"There is no shortage of H_2O on the planet."*

The Earth's Water Supply Is Not in Danger

Rob Lyons

Rob Lyons is commissioning editor at Spiked. *In the following viewpoint, he compares the belief that there is a dire global water shortage, or "peak water," to "peak oil," which, he explains, is the belief that there is only a limited supply of oil available for human use. The notion of peak oil, he says, has been disproved and so will that of peak water. The peak water position came about, Lyons argues, because believers in peak oil were disappointed when forced to come to terms with the reality that there are and will continue to be new sources of oil. Similarly, he says, believers in peak water will be disappointed when they learn that they were wrong. Focusing on the negative, predicting doom and gloom, Lyons argues, are hallmarks of the peak water adherents, and this attitude, he says, precludes finding workable solutions to problems.*

As you read, consider the following questions:

1. What does Lyons say provides greater incentive to develop new technology?

Rob Lyons, "We're Running Out of Water? Get a Grip, Greens," *Spiked*, July 9, 2013. Copyright © 2013 by spiked Ltd. All rights reserved. Reproduced by permission.

41

2. How many cubic miles of freshwater are there on earth, according to the author?

3. Why did Saudi Arabia make a strategic decision to become self-sufficient in wheat production, according to Lyons?

You may have heard of 'peak oil', the notion that the world has a finite supply of oil and at some point the amount coming out of the ground will start to decline. Then, we are assured by gloomy prognosticators, our oil-addicted civilisation will come to an end and we will need to create a new, low-impact society based on using less energy, exclusively generated from renewable sources like wind or solar. The party will soon be over, we're told, with disastrous consequences—though it seems there are quite a few activists and commentators who would pop the cork on a bottle of sparkling elderflower wine if oil ran out and the shit really did hit the fan.

The trouble with the 'peak oil' hypothesis is that events keep proving it wrong. New, untapped fields are found, as happened [in 2013] off the coast of Brazil. More importantly, as oil prices rise, there's a greater incentive to develop new technology. For example, in the US there are both shale gas and shale oil 'revolutions' in progress, where fracking techniques allow gas and oil trapped in rocks to be released. As [British science writer] Matt Ridley noted [in April 2013]: 'After falling for 30 years, US oil production rocketed upwards in the past three years. In 1995, the Bakken field was reckoned by the US Geological Survey to hold a trivial 151 million barrels of recoverable oil. In 2008, this was revised upwards to nearly four billion barrels; two months ago that number was doubled. It is a safe bet that it will be revised upwards again.'

We also get better at using the resources we've got. So cars have become more fuel-efficient, with the best diesel engines now requiring less fuel than trendy hybrid vehicles, like the Toyota Prius. When a resource is free or very cheap, we have little incentive to think about how best to use it; as it becomes more expensive, we either find more of it, use it more smartly, or replace it with something else—or, more likely, we do a combination of those three things.

The Peak Water Alarmists

Disappointed by the failure of the peak-oil disaster to come to fruition, our doom-mongering, Malthusian[1] friends have alighted on other scary narratives to confirm their suspicions of humanity as a rapacious blight on the planet. Their latest is 'peak water'.

On the face of it, peak water is a boneheaded concept on a planet where two thirds of the surface is covered in, er, water. According to the US Geological Survey, there are 332 million cubic miles of water on Earth. What we tend to need, however, is not sea water but fresh water, of which there is much less: nearer 2.5 million cubic miles. And much of that is too deep underground to be accessed. Surface water in rivers and lakes is a small fraction of overall fresh water: 22,339 cubic miles. Handily, though, natural processes cause sea water to evaporate and form clouds, which then dump their contents on to land—so in most populated parts of the world there is currently sufficient water to supply our needs in an endlessly renewable way. As for the future, it is clear there is no shortage of H_2O on the planet. What we really have is a shortage of cheap energy and the necessary technology to take advantage of the salinated stuff.

The 'peak water' theorists focus on groundwater supplies that are either being used faster than they are replenished, or supplies that are not replenished at all: so-called 'fossil water'. According to leading environmentalist Lester Brown, writing in the *Guardian* last weekend [early July 2013], the rapid exhaustion of these supplies in some parts of the world is lead-

---

1. "Malthusian" is a pejorative term used to describe proponents of the theories of eighteenth-century economist Thomas Robert Malthus, who warned of the dangers of overpopulation.

ing to the decline of food production. And at a time of fast-growing populations, this apparently promises disaster for these countries.

A Political, Not Practical, Problem

But often, the problem is a political rather than a practical one. For example, according to Brown, after the Arab oil embargo of the 1970s, Saudi Arabia made a strategic decision to become self-sufficient in wheat to avoid being the victim of a tit-for-tat grain embargo. This largely desert country 'developed a heavily subsidised irrigated agriculture based largely from fossil aquifers', says Brown. Unsurprisingly, those supplies are now running out. Is this a portent of a coming global problem, or just a realisation that growing masses of wheat in a very hot, very dry country is actually impractical, especially when far cheaper supplies of wheat are available from so many sources as to make a successful embargo against Saudi Arabia unlikely?

In reality, all of the fixes that apply to peak oil also apply to peak water. New technology may make water desalination far cheaper than it is now, a claim being made for new water filtration methods based on nanotechnology. Better use of water in irrigation, through careful management of when and how water is applied to crops, could cut usage dramatically—something that is already happening in dry countries such as Israel and Australia and in parts of the US. Current uses of water, like flush toilets, may be superseded in places where water is in high demand. Through civil engineering projects, water can be shifted from places where it is plentiful to places where it is needed most, something societies have been doing for thousands of years.

Environmentalists' Closed Thinking

In other words, what we have is a practical problem, to which people around the world will evolve various solutions that suit their particular circumstances. But such a problem-solving outlook is anathema to environmentalists. Ignore their claim that we are constantly butting up against insuperable problems; it is better to see a natural limit simply as a problem we haven't solved yet. And humanity has an inspiring record of solving problems.

Faith in the future doesn't mean thinking we won't face any serious challenges in that future. Feeding the world when it has an extra two or three billion people won't be straightforward. But experience gives us every reason to believe we have the capacity to accommodate more people living longer, healthier and wealthier lives.

One of the biggest barriers to reaching that goal today is the closed thinking of eco-miserabilists, and the downbeat, green-leaning outlook held by too many political leaders and campaigners. The aim of anyone with the interests of humanity at heart should be to achieve a decline in the influence of such doom-mongers. Peak green, anyone?

Periodical and Internet Sources Bibliography

The following articles have been selected to supplement the diverse views presented in this chapter.

Mike Adams
"The Overpopulation Myth Myth," Infowars, March 15, 2013. www.infowars.com.

Ian Angus
"The Myth of 'Environmental Catastrophism,' " *Monthly Review*, September 2013.

Joel Brinkley
"Iran's Looming Environmental Crisis," *Chicago Tribune*, November 12, 2013.

Hayley Dixon
"Global Warming? No, Actually We're Cooling, Claim Scientists," *Daily Telegraph* (London), September 8, 2013.

Peter Ferrara
"To the Horror of Global Warming Alarmists, Global Cooling Is Here," *Forbes*, May 26, 2013.

Bill Fletcher Jr.
"Addressing the Environmental Crisis Is About More than Recycling," BlackVoiceNews, June 18, 2013. www.blackvoicenews.com.

Dina Fine Maron
"The World Water Shortage Looks Unsolvable," *Salon*, August 4, 2013. www.salon.com.

James Wanliss
"Where's the Real Environmental Crisis?," *Apologia* (blog), November 17, 2013. http://blog.apologia.com.

Tim Worstall
"The Latest Environmental Scare: We're Running Out of Water to Make Burgers With," *Forbes*, June 30, 2013.

Alexis Zeigler
"A Real Answer for the Environmental Crisis: Conscious Cultural Evolution," *Reality Sandwich*, August 19, 2013. http://realitysandwich.com.

CHAPTER 2

How Should Climate Change Be Addressed?

Chapter Preface

On December 4, 2013, the US National Research Council released a report titled "Abrupt Climate Change: Anticipating Surprises," which warns of the potentially catastrophic threat of abrupt impacts of climate change and recommends the implementation of an early warning system that would alert experts to climate "tipping points" so that proactive, rather than reactive, responses can be taken to mitigate or successfully cope with the effects. Rather than emphasizing the gradual warming of the planet, this report focuses upon the uncertainty and instability of the global climate and maintains that it is largely unknown when or precisely how the predicted effects of climate change will manifest themselves.

The report is a follow-up to the group's 2002 report, "Abrupt Climate Change: Inevitable Surprises," and updates the current state of knowledge regarding the potential for abrupt impacts, categorizing various potential events as either highly probable or unlikely. Only two events were rated as likely to occur in the current century: death of coral reefs worldwide and massive melting of Arctic sea ice, both of which could lead to widespread extinction in the affected areas. The report asserts that "the primary timescale of concern is years to decades," and maintains that "Although there is still much to learn about abrupt climate change and abrupt climate impacts, to willfully ignore the threat of abrupt change could lead to more costs, loss of life, suffering, and environmental degradation."

An abrupt change early warning system (ACEWS), the report indicates, would help to minimize the loss of life and destruction of populated or otherwise crucial regions associated with a catastrophic abrupt change in the climate. John Timmer of the online publication *Ars Technica* explains that such a warning system "would involve a group that identifies systems where abrupt climate change is a risk and directs research into the factors that control the behavior of these systems, as well as how their behavior changes as it approaches a tipping point. The group would also identify the human infrastructure and ecosystems that would be most vulnerable to sudden changes." But according to Richard Harris, reporting in 2013 for National Public Radio, "The proposal to deal with these rapid changes faces a steep road ahead. Key Republicans in Congress are currently trying to slash money for climate research, not add to it."

An ACEWS is just one among dozens of recommendations that scientists and policy makers have made for addressing the multitude of effects that climate change could have on the world. In the viewpoints in this chapter, authors provide different perspectives on the relative merits of and best ways of implementing possible solutions to slow or even erase the effects of climate change, including the use of renewable and nuclear energy and reducing carbon emissions.

> "[Renewable energy] is playing an important role in climate mitigation strategies."

Renewable Energy Can Significantly Reduce the Impact of Climate Change

Intergovernmental Panel on Climate Change

The Intergovernmental Panel on Climate Change (IPCC) is an intergovernmental body established in 1988 by the World Meteorological Organization and the United Nations Environment Programme to provide policy makers with authoritative and objective scientific and technical assessments. In the following viewpoint, the IPCC argues that the use of renewable energy sources greatly reduces the carbon emissions that are responsible for increasing global temperatures and thus should be used to replace carbon-producing energy sources such as fossil fuels. Paired with technologies and policies that reduce energy use and intensity, the IPCC contends, renewable energy sources can provide tremendous cost savings and increased energy efficiency. In addition to reducing carbon emissions, the IPCC maintains, renew-

able energy yields improvements in global health (due to reductions in pollution and access to services), social and economic development, increased access to energy, and greater energy security. The author provides numerous examples of how renewable energy has been implemented successfully around the world, and how government policies are shaped by existing renewable energy technology.

As you read, consider the following questions:

1. What does the IPCC say would have to happen for all vehicles on the planet to be run on biofuels?

2. According to the author, how many people, around the world lacked access to electricity in 2009?

3. How many European municipalities had joined the Covenant of Mayors by March 2010, according to the IPCC?

Renewable energy [RE] is any form of energy from solar, geophysical or biological sources that is replenished by natural processes at a rate that equals or exceeds its rate of use. RE is obtained from the continuing or repetitive flows of energy occurring in the natural environment and includes resources such as biomass, solar energy, geothermal heat, hydropower, tide and waves and ocean thermal energy, and wind energy. However, it is possible to utilize biomass at a greater rate than it can grow, or to draw heat from a geothermal field at a faster rate than heat flows can replenish it. On the other hand, the rate of utilization of direct solar energy has no bearing on the rate at which it reaches the Earth. Fossil fuels (coal, oil, natural gas) do not fall under this definition, as they are not replenished within a time frame that is short relative to their rate of utilization.

There is a multi-step process whereby primary energy is converted into an energy carrier (heat, electricity or mechanical work), and then into an energy service. RE technologies are diverse and can serve the full range of energy service needs. Various types of RE can supply electricity, thermal energy and mechanical energy, as well as produce fuels that are able to satisfy multiple energy service needs.

Since it is energy services and not energy that people need, the goal is to meet those needs in an efficient manner that requires less primary energy consumption with low-carbon technologies that minimize CO_2 [carbon dioxide] emissions. . . .

Energy Savings and Renewable Energy

Energy services are the tasks to be performed using energy. A specific energy service can be provided in many ways. Lighting, for example, may be provided by daylight, candles or oil lamps or by a multitude of different electric lamps. The efficiency of the multiple conversions of energy from primary source to final output may be high or low, and may involve the release of large or small amounts of CO_2 (under a given energy mix). Hence there are many options as to how to supply any particular service. . . .

Energy savings arise from decreasing energy intensity by changing the activities that demand energy inputs. For example, turning off lights when not needed, walking instead of taking vehicular transportation, changing the controls for heating or air conditioning to avoid excessive heating or cooling or eliminating a particular appliance and performing a task in a less energy intensive manner are all examples of energy savings. Energy savings can be realized by technical, organizational, institutional and structural changes and by changed behaviour.

Studies suggest that energy savings resulting from efficiency measures are not always fully realized in practice. There may be a rebound effect in which some fraction of the measure is offset because the lower total cost of energy to perform a specific energy service may lead to utilization of more energy services. Rebound effects can be distinguished at the micro and macro level. At the micro level, a successful energy efficiency measure may be expected to lead to lower energy costs for the entity subject to the measure because it uses less energy. However, the full energy saving may not occur because a more efficient vehicle reduces the cost of operation per kilometre, so the user may drive more kilometres. Or a better-insulated home may not achieve the full saving because it is now possible to achieve greater comfort by using some of the saved energy. . . .

Increasing Energy Efficiency

The role of energy efficiency in combination with RE is somewhat more complex and less studied. It is necessary to examine the total cost of end-use efficiency measures plus RE technology, and then determine whether there is rebound effect for a specific case.

Furthermore, carbon leakage may also reduce the effectiveness of carbon reduction policies. Carbon leakage is defined as the increase in CO_2 emissions outside of the countries taking domestic mitigation action divided by the reduction in the emissions of these countries. If carbon reduction policies are not applied uniformly across sectors and political jurisdictions, then it is possible for carbon-emitting activities that are controlled in one place to move to another sector or country where such activities are not restricted. Recent research suggests, however, that estimates of carbon leakage are too high.

Reducing energy needed at the energy service delivery stage is an important means of reducing the primary energy required for all energy supply fuels and technologies. Because RE sources usually have a lower power density than fossil or nuclear fuels, energy savings at the end-use stage are often required to utilize a RE technology for a specific energy service. For example, it may not be possible to fuel all vehicles on the planet with biofuels at their current low engine efficiencies, but if vehicle fuel efficiency were greater, a larger fraction of vehicles could be run on biofuels. Similarly, by lowering demand, the size and cost of a distributed solar system may become competitive. The importance of end-use efficiency in buildings in order for renewable technology to be a viable option has been documented. Furthermore, electricity distribution and management is simplified and system balancing costs are lower if the energy demands are smaller. Energy efficiency at the end-use stage thus facilitates the use of RE. . . .

Opportunities for Renewable Energy

Opportunities can be defined as circumstances for action with the attribute of a chance character. In the policy context, that could be the anticipation of additional benefits that may go along with the deployment of RE . . . but that are not intentionally targeted. There are four major opportunity areas that RE is well suited to address. . . . The four areas are social and economic development, energy access, energy security, and climate change mitigation and the reduction of environmental and health impacts.

Social and Economic Development

Globally, per capita incomes as well as broader indicators such as the Human Development Index are positively correlated with per capita energy use, and economic growth can be identified as the most relevant factor behind increasing energy consumption in the last decades. As economic activity expands and diversifies, demands for more sophisticated and flexible energy sources arise. Economic development has therefore been associated with a shift from direct combustion of fuels to higher quality electricity.

Particularly for developing countries, the link between social and economic development and the need for modern energy services is evident. Access to clean and reliable energy constitutes an important prerequisite for fundamental determinants of human development, contributing, inter alia [among other things], to economic activity, income generation, poverty alleviation, health, education and gender equality. Because of their decentralized nature, RE technologies can play an important role in fostering rural development.

The creation of (new) employment opportunities is seen as a positive long-term effect of RE both in developed and developing countries and was stressed in many national green-growth strategies. Also, policymakers have supported the development of domestic markets for RE as a means to gain competitive advantage in supplying international markets.

Increased Energy Access

In 2009, more than 1.4 billion people globally lacked access to electricity, 85% of them in rural areas, and the number of people relying on traditional biomass for cooking was estimated to be around 2.7 billion. By 2015, almost 1.2 billion more people will need access to electricity and 1.9 billion more people will need access to modern fuels to meet the Millennium Development Goal of halving the proportion of people living in poverty [by 2015].

The transition to modern energy access is referred to as moving up the energy ladder and implies a progression from traditional to more modern devices/fuels that are more environmentally benign and have fewer negative health impacts. Various initiatives, some of them based on RE, particularly in the developing countries, aim at improving universal access to modern energy services through increased access to electricity and cleaner cooking facilities. In particular, reliance on RE in rural applications, use of locally produced bioenergy to produce electricity, and access to clean cooking facilities will contribute to attainment of universal access to modern energy services.

For electricity, small and stand-alone configurations of RE technologies such as PV [photo-voltaics, or solar energy panels], hydropower, and bioenergy can often meet energy needs of rural communities more cheaply than fossil fuel alternatives such as diesel generators. For example, PV is attractive as a source of electric power to provide basic services, such as lighting and clean drinking water. For greater local demand, small-scale hydropower or biomass combustion and [coal] gasification technologies may offer better solutions. For bioenergy, the progression implies moving from the use of, for example, firewood, cow dung and agricultural residues to, for example, liquid propane gas stoves, RE-based advanced biomass cookstoves or biogas systems.

Greater Energy Security

At a general level, energy security can best be understood as robustness against (sudden) disruptions of energy supply. More specifically, availability and distribution of resources, as well as variability and reliability of energy supply, can be identified as the two main themes.

Current energy supplies are dominated by fossil fuels (petroleum and natural gas) whose price volatility can have significant impacts, in particular for oil-importing developing countries. National security concerns about the geopolitical availability of fuels have also been a major driver for a number of countries to consider RE. For example, in the USA, the military has led the effort to expand and diversify fuel supplies for aviation and cites improved energy supply security as the major driving force for sustainable alternative fuels. . . .

Climate Change Mitigation

Climate change mitigation is one of the key driving forces behind a growing demand for RE technologies. In addition to reducing GHG [greenhouse gas] emissions, RE technologies can also offer benefits with respect to air pollution and health compared to fossil fuels. . . .

The Role of Renewable Energy in Reducing Carbon Emissions

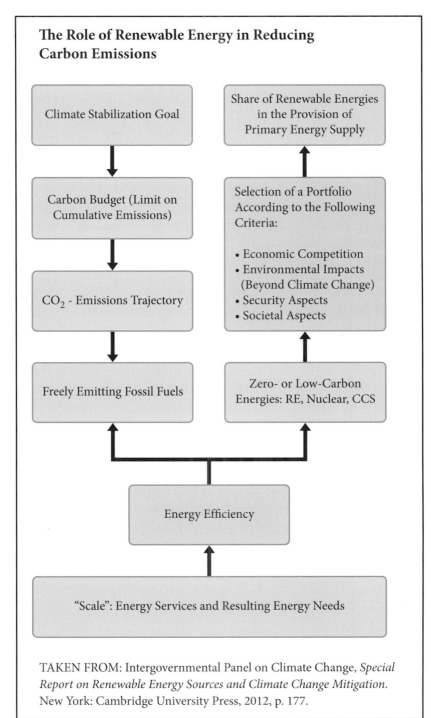

TAKEN FROM: Intergovernmental Panel on Climate Change, *Special Report on Renewable Energy Sources and Climate Change Mitigation*. New York: Cambridge University Press, 2012, p. 177.

Traditional biomass use results in health impacts from the high concentrations of particulate matter and carbon monoxide, among other pollutants. Long-term exposure to biomass smoke increases the risk of a child developing an acute respiratory infection and is a major cause of morbidity and mortality in developing countries.

In this context, non-combustion-based RE power generation technologies have the potential to significantly reduce local and regional air pollution and lower associated health impacts compared to fossil-based power generation. Improving traditional biomass use can reduce negative impacts on sustainable development, including local and indoor air pollution, GHG emissions, deforestation and forest degradation.

Impacts on water resources from energy systems strongly depend on technology choice and local conditions. Electricity production with wind and solar PV, for example, requires very little water compared to thermal conversion technologies, and has no impacts on water quality. Limited water availability for cooling thermal power plants decreases their efficiency, which can affect plants operating on coal, biomass, gas, nuclear and concentrating solar power. There have been significant power reductions from nuclear and coal plants during drought conditions in the USA and France in recent years.

Surface-mined coal in particular produces major alterations of land; coal mines can create acid mine drainage and the storage of coal ash can contaminate surface and ground waters. Oil production and transportation have led to significant land and water spills. Most renewable technologies produce lower conventional air and water pollutants than fossil fuels, but may require large amounts of land as, for example, reservoir hydropower (which can also release methane from submerged vegetation), wind energy and biofuels.

Since a degree of climate change is now inevitable, adaptation to climate change is an essential component of sustainable development. Adaptation can be either anticipatory or reactive to an altered climate. Some RE technologies may assist in adapting to change, and are usually anticipatory in nature. . . .

- Active and passive solar cooling of buildings helps counter the direct impacts on humans of rising mean temperatures;

- Dams (used for hydropower) may also be important in managing the impacts of droughts and floods, which are projected to increase with climate change. Indeed, this is one of reasons for building such dams in the first place;

- Solar PV and wind require no water for their operation, and hence may become increasingly important as droughts and high river temperatures limit the power output of thermal power plants;

- Water pumps in rural areas remote from the power grid can utilize PV or wind for raising agricultural productivity during climate-induced increases in dry seasons and droughts; and

- Tree planting and forest preservation along coasts and riverbanks is a key strategy for lessening the coastal erosion impacts of climate change. With suitable choice of species and silvicultural [forestry] practices, these plantings can also yield a sustainable source of biomass for energy, for example, by coppicing [frequent cutting of young trees to encourage greater growth]. . . .

Renewable Energy and Government Policy

RE is an integral aspect of government strategies for reducing CO_2 (and other) emissions in many countries, including all member states of the EU [European Union]; and several US states, including California and Washington. Developing countries are also enacting RE policies in order to address climate change, among other goals. India's National Action Plan on Climate Change, launched in 2008, specifically mentions RE, and the country's National Solar Mission aims to constitute a major contribution by India to the global effort to meet the challenges of climate change. The 2009 meeting of Leaders of Pacific Island Countries observed that in addition to RE offering the promise of cost-effective, reliable energy services to rural households it will also provide a contribution to global GHG mitigation efforts.

In numerous cities, from Chicago and Miami in the USA to Rizhao in China and Waitakere in New Zealand, RE is playing an important role in climate mitigation strategies. By March 2010, more than 1,300 European municipalities had joined the Covenant of Mayors, committing to reduce CO_2 emissions beyond the EU objective of 20% by 2020 with the help of RE deployment, among other tools.

The benefits of RE to the broader environment and human health are also driving governments to enact RE policies. At the same time, manufacture, construction and disposal of RE systems can have direct non-climate change impacts on the natural environment, including land use and aesthetics, and problems associated with chemicals required for manufacture and others. Policymakers can implement processes to minimize these negative outcomes while benefiting from the opportunities and benefits. . . .

In China, for example, a major driver for the promotion of clean energy technologies, including RE, has been the goal of reducing or avoiding negative local and regional environmental impacts associated with energy. The government of Pakistan intends to develop RE in order to avoid local environmental and health impacts of unsustainable and inefficient traditional biomass fuels and fossil fuel-powered electricity generation. The South African government recognizes that millions of people are routinely exposed to noxious gases and particulates from the burning of fossil fuels due to inadequate living conditions and a lack of infrastructure in much of the country; the need to improve air quality has been a motivating factor in government plans to deploy RE technologies. In light of increasing concerns about water scarcity, many governments are turning to RE to reduce water consumption associated with energy production.

Growing awareness of the potential for RE to avoid some of the harmful impacts of fuel extraction on biodiversity of plant and animal species has led some governments to establish targets, or to adopt other policies, to increase RE deployment. For example, the Commonwealth of the Bahamas pays special attention to RE technology as a means to sustain vulnerable ecosystem services. In Nepalese villages, modern RE systems have been deployed to mitigate negative impacts on biodiversity and deforestation resulting from the unsustainable use of biomass.

> "Far from a realistic plan, the [National
> Renewable Energy Lab] study suggests
> what might be possible in an ideal
> world."

Renewable Energy's Role in Reducing Climate Change Is Currently Limited

Matthew Stepp

Matthew Stepp is a contributing writer at Renewable Energy
World *and a senior policy analyst at the Information Technology
and Innovation Foundation. In the following viewpoint, Stepp
argues that a study published by the National Renewable Energy
Laboratory (NREL) does not, in fact, indicate that renewable energy is sufficient to solve problems from climate change and
high-carbon energy sources such as fossil fuel, contrary to the
claims of several renewable energy advocates who claim that it
does. Stepp contends that conclusions drawn from the study are
not based on real-world conditions; in fact, he asserts, in order
to achieve the goal of supplying even half of the amount of the
US power supply with solar and wind energy the United States
would have to first create massive hydrostorage, stop increases in*

energy demand, and double the current US transmission system. To ensure that renewable energy sources can contribute significantly to reduce carbon emissions and impact climate change, he concludes, considerable investments must first be made in technology to support its expanded use and a diverse energy profile: better energy storage, more efficient and less expensive wind and solar options, better carbon capture and storage, and safer nuclear power.

As you read, consider the following questions:

1. By what percentage does Stepp say California's energy demands have increased in the past twenty years?

2. According to the author, what percentage of the planet's energy is provided by fossil fuels?

3. Stepp says US investment in energy innovation is less than 5 percent of what?

We're losing the race against global warming. Worldwide coal production increased about eight times faster than solar- and wind-power generation last year [2012]. China added more new coal plants in 2011 than are running in Texas and Ohio, even as it leads the world in wind-power capacity. Meanwhile, the United States is only modestly cutting carbon emissions by transitioning from coal to natural gas, which is still a carbon-rich fuel.

Despite these trends, conventional wisdom holds that a "clean-energy future" is not only possible but looming. Through a combination of energy efficiency and renewable technologies, some argue, we can "solve" the problem of climate change.

The case for "we've got all the renewables we need" recently received a boost from a National Renewable Energy Laboratory (NREL) study, which concluded: "Renewable electricity generation from technologies that are commercially available today, in combination with a more flexible electric system, is more than adequate to supply 80% of total U.S. electricity generation in 2050 while meeting electricity demand on an hourly basis in every region of the country." Physicist Amory Lovins, a leading advocate of green energy, was among those praising the study. It showed "how to produce 80 to 90 percent of America's electricity from proven, reliable and increasingly competitive renewable sources like the sun and wind," he said.

Yet on close reading, the study not only doesn't support these optimistic claims, it also reveals the need for a more diverse technology strategy and aggressive investments in innovation.

Current Renewable Energy Technology Is Not Possible in the Real World

For starters, the study doesn't find that wind and solar can, even theoretically, supply 80 to 90 percent of U.S. power by 2050. In the best case, less than half would come from wind and sun. The remaining balance of renewable power would come from new hydropower, equivalent to adding 50 Hoover-size dams and building biomass plants equal in capacity to the U.S. nuclear fleet; the biomass plants are unlikely to be carbon-neutral.

Even achieving the goal of 50 percent of the U.S. power supply from solar and wind assumes that 100 to 150 gigawatts of energy storage, or roughly half the size of the country's coal capacity, will emerge to provide power when the sun isn't shining and the wind isn't blowing. While pumped hydro-storage is available in some locations today, other technology options, such as very large batteries and compressed air, require significantly more innovation to become cost-effective at commercial scale.

In fact, the study's storage estimate may be low, because it assumes that the number of residences and businesses that will go offline at peak times when wind and solar aren't available are equivalent to 1 1/2 New York states. It also assumes no growth in U.S. electric consumption for the next 40 years, thanks to improvement in energy efficiency. Consider that California's energy-efficiency efforts lead the world—but demand has still increased 25 percent in the Golden State in the past 20 years.

Furthermore, to meet the goal of having 50 percent of the U.S. power supply come from solar and wind sources, the study presumes a doubling of the U.S. transmission system that is simply not feasible. Nearly every mile of new U.S. transmission lines is fought over by the localities they run through. And the report is mum on what happens to electricity reliability or consumer costs if more than one of these assumptions fails to materialize.

Simply put: Far from a realistic plan, the NREL study suggests what might be possible in an ideal world. The authors even admit that although their analysis suggests "a high renewable generation future is possible, a transformation of the electricity system would need to occur . . . involving every element of the grid."

Investing in New Technology Research

Certainly, better efficiency and increased wind and solar power will be among the ways to address global warming. But placing all of our bets on today's renewable technologies is unwise. A more sensible approach would be to invest in improving the performance and cost of a broad range of zero-carbon technologies through innovation, including better and cheaper wind and solar power as well as energy storage.

We must also be realistic about fossil fuels, which provide 87 percent of the planet's energy and aren't disappearing anytime soon. The United States needs to bring commercially proven carbon capture and storage to scale and reduce its cost. It also would be prudent to explore cheaper next-generation nuclear technologies that offer better safety, waste and security options than the Fukushima-type light-water designs that were locked in during the [President Dwight D.] Eisenhower administration.

The real lesson of the NREL study is that much more innovation is necessary to achieve deep and affordable carbon reductions. Yet almost all of the policy and funding today focuses on deploying current technologies. U.S. investment in energy innovation is less than 5 percent of federal spending on defense research and demonstration. That has to change. We need better, cheaper options if the grid is to produce less carbon.

> *"Nuclear fission is the only known technology capable of bringing CO_2 emissions under control."*

Nuclear Power Is the Best Way to Address Climate Change

Arthur R. Williams

Arthur R. Williams is a writer, patent agent, condensed-matter theorist, and retired from a thirty-year career with the IBM Thomas J. Watson Research Center. In the following viewpoint, Williams argues that nuclear energy is the best and only clean energy source that has a realistic chance of being utilized on a scale large enough to combat climate change. He claims that there are six "myths," or misconceptions about nuclear energy and other forms of renewable energy that have kept nuclear from being embraced by environmentalists as a solution to global warming: 1) wind and solar energy are sufficient energy sources; 2) nuclear energy is dangerous; 3) there are no safe ways or places to store nuclear waste; 4) nuclear energy is insufficient to address the issues of transportation and clean water; 5) nuclear energy plants are too large and expensive, and it is difficult to find locations to build them; and 6) more or even "game-changing" technology must be developed before nuclear could be

*safe or commercially viable. Williams refutes these myths, ex-
plaining that nuclear fission can be applied to fuel vehicles using
ammonia synthesis, and asserting that not only are nuclear energy and nuclear waste storage safe, they can be made much
safer with recent advances such as molten-salt reactors and
waste reduction technology. Furthermore, he concludes, wind
and solar energy technology are in early phases of development
and therefore expensive and inefficient while nuclear energy is a
mature technology that is both cost-effective and efficient and
thus the only viable solution to fight global warming.*

As you read, consider the following questions:

1. As cited by Williams, how many minutes of electricity
   consumption does Bill Gates say can be stored by all the
   world's existing batteries?

2. What percentage of France's electricity has been produced from nuclear fission, according to Williams?

3. How many fission facilities does the author say are under construction in China?

Global warming, energy independence, water scarcity and
third-world economic growth are all amenable to a common, safe, clean, cost-competitive and field-tested nuclear solution. Why isn't this solution universally embraced and implemented?

I suggest two reasons. First, we humans respond much
more strongly to dramatic events, like earthquakes, violent
weather and terrorist acts, than we do to steady-state threats,
such as auto accidents, medical errors and coal particles. At a
cost of $4 trillion, we started two wars in response to the ter-
rorist attacks of 9/11 that killed 2,996. The death tolls in the
US from auto accidents (30,000), medical errors (44,000–
200,000), and coal dust (13,000) are not only higher, but also
perennial. The gradual character of carbon dioxide emissions
and global warming is elevating our "boiling frog" tendencies

to an entirely new scale of danger. Although the problem may not excite us, our pot is warming so quickly that we must leap [like a frog in a pot of heating water] to survive.

Greater Practicality and Myth Busting

A measure of the magnitude and urgency of this challenge can be found in Bill Gates' summary of his wonderful TED [Technology Education Design] lecture on this topic: Despite the time, effort and money he has devoted to new vaccines and seeds, if he could be granted a single wish for the coming decades, it would be for a practical, CO_2-free energy source. That explicit prioritization reflects his awareness of an especially unfortunate feature of warming, that its burden falls most heavily on the politically voiceless poor, and less heavily on those with the means to address the challenge. The disparity adds to our inertia.

The second reason lies in deeply entrenched myths (which for my purposes I shall define as untruths breeding complacency), rooted in unrealistically high expectations for renewable energy and unrealistically negative expectations for nuclear power. Criticism of nuclear power focuses on history and ignores dramatic advances in fission technology. This incomplete picture gives rise to myths that conflict directly with the assertions of Gates and of John Parmentola, the US army's director of research and laboratory management: that nuclear fission is the only "practical" solution in view.

The remainder of this essay comments on Gates' criteria for "practicality," and examines the factors of availability, reliability, cost, scale, safety, proliferation and waste. The good news is that new fission technologies make fission clean, safe, competitively inexpensive, and resistant to terrorism. Moreover, they solve the nuclear-waste challenge. One technology claims to reduce the high-level waste output of a typical power plant from 20 tons per year to a few kilograms. American startups are pursuing commercialization, but much of the action is in other countries, notably China and India.

Gates and Parmentola also emphasize the urgency for halting CO_2 emissions. In my view, the following six widespread and paralyzing myths must be addressed.

Myth #1

Wind and solar can do it. Renewable sources, like wind, solar, and tide, emit no CO_2, and that's undeniably good. While the discussion of renewables often focuses on cost, it is power density and intermittency that conspire with cost to prevent these technologies from providing adequate solutions.

As Gates puts it, technologies for renewable energy represent energy farming. Because the intrinsic power density of renewable sources is orders of magnitude lower than that of hydrocarbons and nuclear processes, large tracts of land are required to reap even modest quantities of power.

Even if large tracts of land, such as those in the Sahara or the American Southwest, are employed, the electricity produced is inherently intermittent, and must be stored and transported. For example, Gates estimates that all the world's existing batteries can store only about 10 minutes of electricity consumption. Also, because land is not available near population centers, transport such as high-tension towers must be provided.

While the relative cost of renewable sources is improving, cost still represents a disadvantage of several hundred percent that has been compensated by government subsidies. Subsidies might continue, but as [Robert] Hargraves emphasizes in his extensively researched book, *Thorium: Energy Cheaper than Coal*, the prospects for eliminating CO_2 emissions are greatly improved if the alternative power source is cheaper than hydrocarbons. The high energy density and availability of coal make it misleadingly attractive. Hargraves concludes that at least one of the next-generation breed-and-burn fission technologies can produce electricity for about \$0.03/kWh, making it cost-competitive, even with coal. The intrinsic safety and relative simplicity of the coming generation of breed-and-burn fission reactors makes them significantly less expensive than those of the present generation.

Myth #2

Nuclear is unsafe. There are two safety issues in the context of nuclear power: meltdown and terrorism. Both are essentially eliminated by next-generation fission technologies.

Concerns raised by incidents at Three Mile Island and Chernobyl were seriously aggravated by recent events at Fukushima. Such dangers are not intrinsic to fission, but stem from military priorities favoring fuel rods comprised of metal-clad ceramics. Ceramics conduct heat poorly, and active cooling (powered externally) is required to prevent overheating, melting and rupture of the cladding. Molten-salt reactors are qualitatively different. First, exploiting the molten state leads to an inherently safe reactor design, since no additional melting is possible. More specifically, the far superior thermal conductivity of molten salt eliminates the need for active cooling. At any time and without any external power, the reactor can be drained, by gravity, into a subterranean vessel in which passive cooling suffices. Such reactors are termed "walk-away" safe. A molten-salt reactor ran successfully and without incident at Oak Ridge National Laboratory for four years.

High-level wastes produced by fission are unavoidable, but they are only a tiny fraction of what we call nuclear waste. The complete burning of nuclear fuel in molten-salt reactors provides all the benefits of reprocessing, which has permitted France, for example, to produce about 80% of its electricity from fission for decades, without theft of fissile material by terrorists, although [environmentalist group] Greenpeace did block a plutonium shipment. Because next-generation reactors integrate breeding and burning into a single process, fissile material does not exist outside the reactor, where it is both hot and diluted, thereby reducing the risk of theft significantly below even that of reprocessing.

Myth #3

Nuclear waste remains an unsolved problem. As the term "breed-and-burn" suggests, next-generation fission technologies are related to and provide the benefits of reprocessing. An independent benefit of molten-salt technologies is that the fissile material can remain in the reactor until it is completely consumed, thereby producing dramatically less waste. In today's solid-fuel reactors the fuel is clad in metals that can tolerate only a limited amount of neutron bombardment, necessitating removal of the fuel long before it is fully consumed. This distinction is the basis of the claim by the MIT [Massachusetts Institute of Technology]-based startup, Transatomic Power, that waste production can be reduced from tons to kilograms, increasing by a factor of 30 the energy obtained from a given quantity of fuel. Refueling frequency is also reduced in molten-salt reactors by the continuous removal of neutron-absorbing xenon, whose accumulation in solid-fuel reactors also reduces the time that fuel can remain in the reactor.

A bonus, but not a surprise, given the connection between breed-and-burn reactors and reprocessing, is that some new reactors can consume existing nuclear waste—both depleted and spent fuel. In this way, next-generation fission can solve the waste problem created by present-generation fission.

Myth #4

Fission may provide electricity, but it does not fuel transportation or provide clean water. Fission produces cheap heat, which is broadly useful. In the present context, the cost-effective heat produced by fission is symbiotic with two highly developed technologies that address two of our most critical challenges, CO_2-free transportation and seawater desalination.

Transportation consumes a large fraction of the energy budget. Its fractional share is approaching that of industry, which is about twice that of both residential and commercial energy consumption. Since fission reactors are unlikely to be placed in cars and trucks, in what sense can fission contribute to CO_2-free transportation? The answer is the synthesis of ammonia [NH_3]. NH_3 synthesis is among the most promising exploitations of heat from fission. NH_3 can be viewed as an especially effective medium for hydrogen storage and delivery. The infrastructure for NH_3 production and distribution is already widespread. NH_3 has about half the energy content by weight of gasoline, but its much lower cost gives it a price-performance advantage. Most importantly, NH_3 burns to form air and water:

$$4NH_3 + 3O_2 = 2N_2 + 6H_2O$$

Fission also offers a choice between electrically powered reverse osmosis and traditional distillation as means to produce potable water. Distillation can use fission-produced heat directly, whereas reverse osmosis is very energy demanding, and can use fission-produced electricity. Either way, the value of potable water is rising rapidly, and will benefit directly from cheap clean power.

Myth #5

Nuclear installations are large, expensive and problematic to site. The greater efficiency of molten-salt reactors makes them smaller for a given capacity. More importantly, they operate at atmospheric pressure, which eliminates both the threat of explosion and the need for a large containment structure, the visual signature of today's fission plants. In combination with the pervasive relative simplicity of molten-fuel reactors, elimination of the containment structure renders molten-salt facili-

Fukushima Proves That Nuclear Power Is Safe

Every energy technology carries a cost; so does the absence of energy technologies. Atomic energy has just been subjected to one of the harshest of possible tests, and the impact on people and the planet has been small. The [March 2011] crisis at Fukushima has converted me to the cause of nuclear power.

George Monbiot,
Guardian (Manchester, UK), March 21, 2011.

ties relatively small and inexpensive. Such reactors also lend themselves to factory manufacture, further reducing their cost. The original molten-fuel reactor was intended to power airplanes. In the present context, the efficiency, reduced size, and guaranteed safety of next-generation fission plants combine to reduce the NIMBY (not in my backyard) resistance to their siting.

Myth #6

Nuclear requires lengthy development. Writing in the February 2013 issue of *Physics Today*, John Parmentola called for the invention of a game-changing fission technology. Correspondingly, Gates calls for hundreds of startups pursuing different variations on the common theme. Gates is involved with one such company, TerraPower, which will commercialize an innovative solid-fuel breed-and-burn technology.

The call for startups and game changers reveals the great irony of this context: that arguably the most promising of the breed-and-burn technologies is not at all new. As mentioned above, the molten-salt thorium reactor was developed at Oak Ridge National Lab in the 1960s, where it ran successfully for four years.

A measure of the significance of the Oak Ridge effort is the conviction and enthusiasm of the Oak Ridge lab director, Alvin Weinberg. His zeal for the intrinsic safety and other virtues of the molten-salt reactor, now called LFTR (lithium-fluoride thorium reactor), was not politically welcome, and led to his firing by President [Richard] Nixon in 1973. Weinberg devoted the rest of his life to the promotion of LFTR; the Weinberg Foundation continues his mission.

A contemporary proponent of LFTR, Kirk Sorensen, leads the startup Flibe, which is focused on LFTR commercialization. The MIT-based startup Transatomic Power recently won an ARPA-E [Advanced Research Projects Agency-Energy] competition as part of its efforts to commercialize an LFTR-related technology that will burn "spent" fuel or uranium, at least initially.

Where the Action Is

As David Kramer reported in the November 2012 issue of *Physics Today*, enthusiasm for nuclear power has waned in the US. The Fukushima events have led to similar declines in Japan and Germany. Fortunately for the world, others are moving forward; consider fission facilities in China:

14 operational

27 under construction

51 planned

120 proposed

212 total

The central assertion here echoes that of both Gates and Parmentola: nuclear fission is the only known technology capable of bringing CO_2 emissions under control. My hope is that greater awareness of the benefits promised by coming fission technologies will debunk the myths currently stalling public and private investment, and reverse the unfortunate trend in the US, Japan and Germany.

| "Nuclear power is an unnecessary cost burden on energy consumers ... [and] has led to costly accidents which dwarf the scale of other forms of generation."

Nuclear Power Is an Environmentally and Economically Unsound Way to Address Climate Change

Friends of the Earth

Friends of the Earth is a nonprofit organization that advocates for food and water safety, conservation and protection of wildlife and natural habitats, clean energy, and solutions to fight climate change. In the following viewpoint, Friends of the Earth declares that the British government's plan to expand the use of nuclear energy is wrong-headed and should be abandoned. Rather than encourage energy companies to build new nuclear reactors, the author contends, the government should promote electricity conservation and focus on reducing pollution. A sound combination of renewable energy sources like wind, solar, and hydropower, the Friends of the Earth asserts, could supply the vast majority of Britain's electricity needs while realizing greater cost savings and carbon reductions than using nuclear power. In addition, the author notes, such renewable energy sources do not carry the risks of nuclear energy: nuclear disasters in the form of reactor meltdowns or radioactive waste leaks are not only costly in terms of human lives but in dollars spent on cleanup and lost when economies are devastated. Those who claim that nuclear energy is less expensive than renewable energy, the Friends of the Earth concludes, are simply wrong: Nuclear energy is far more expensive to run, and radioactive waste is not only expensive to store, it cannot be stored safely.

As you read, consider the following questions:

1. What is the decarbonization goal for 2030 in kilowatts per hour of electricity, according to the Friends of the Earth?

2. What does the author say was described as the biggest construction project in Europe?

3. How many people were evacuated following the Chernobyl disaster, according to the author?

In coming decades Britain's nuclear power stations are due to close and, in Friends of the Earth's opinion, they should not be replaced. New nuclear plants are not needed to keep the lights on. They are also not needed to contribute to carbon pollution reductions. Nuclear power also brings unique risks not faced by other energy technologies such as long-lived radioactive waste management.

The cost of new nuclear power stations is rapidly increasing. Meanwhile the costs of many renewable technologies such as onshore wind and solar PV [photovoltaics, or solar energy panels] are falling rapidly, with significant cost reductions possible for new technologies like offshore wind.

Despite being a 60 year old industry, new nuclear power can only be built in Britain with huge public subsidies. This will divert funding away from renewable energy and energy saving. It will also fail to provide best value for money for consumers. Subsidising nuclear power would break commitments from the Conservative, Liberal Democrat and Labour parties.

Friends of the Earth believes the Government should abandon its plans for new nuclear power and instead focus efforts on energy saving, renewable energy and energy storage.

Far-Fetched Nuclear Plans

The Government is encouraging energy companies to build new nuclear power plants. The Government claims this is necessary because demand for electricity will soar as more people power their heating and transport electrically and because some existing power stations are expected to be shut down, including every existing nuclear station. . . .

A recent analysis for the Government suggests that, without action on energy efficiency, electricity demand could grow to up to 470 TWh [terawatt (trillion-watt) hours] per year by 2030, compared with around 370 TWh in 2010 as a result of underlying growth and electrification of transport and heating. However the analysis also showed the potential to constrain this demand to less than 400 TWh through energy efficiency measures in homes, commerce and industry. However, even if electricity demand did grow to 470 TWh we would still be able to produce this electricity without needing new nuclear power stations (see below).

The Government wants new nuclear power plants to be built to replace nuclear power plants that are due to close down over the next decade or so, and increase the amount of electricity from nuclear power from 60 TWh currently to 103 TWh by 2030. The pro-nuclear Birmingham Policy Commission said in their recent report on nuclear energy that even to maintain current levels of nuclear electricity by 2035 would require "*outstanding effectiveness of government policy above and beyond the performance to date"*. The nuclear industry also has a poor record of constructing plants on time and on budget, with very significant delays and escalating costs in France and Finland. The only way any nuclear plants will be built is if the government provides huge subsidies—that would go onto consumers' energy bills for decades ahead—and even then it is highly unlikely that more than a few could be constructed in the timetable the government suggests. Friends of the Earth opposes this long-term subsidy arrangement for a mature technology like nuclear power. Subsidies should be time limited and focused on developing and bringing to market relatively new technologies such as offshore wind.

The Government's plans are not just far-fetched. They could also put at risk future carbon pollution reduction targets agreed by the Coalition Government under the Climate Change Act 2008. This is because by ploughing ahead with a far-fetched idea that eight new nuclear plants will be built, and built on time, the Government may not put enough effort into renewables or energy saving. This could lead to a situation where faster to build unabated gas-fired stations are built instead. Chancellor George Osborne has already spoken out in favour of a major 'dash for gas'. The Committee on Climate Change has already warned that this would wreck the chance of delivering carbon targets and the 2030 decarbonisation goal ($50g$ CO_2 [carbon dioxide] per KWhr [kilowatt hours] of electricity).

New Nuclear Plants Are Not Needed

The Government claims new nuclear power plants are needed to meet electricity needs while meeting carbon emissions targets. Yet Britain can meet its power needs and its carbon targets without nuclear power.

Britain has abundant renewable energy resources which could be exploited instead, as well as substantial untapped potential for energy efficiency. The Offshore Valuation Group says our practical off-shore energy resource exceeds our current electricity consumption six times over.

Even advocates of nuclear power admit that nuclear power doesn't have to be part of the energy mix. Professor Dave Mackay, DECC's [Department of Energy and Climate Change's] Chief Scientific Advisor, says "No-nuclear pathways are certainly technically possible" and the Energy Secretary, Ed Davey, says Britain can survive without nuclear.

The European Climate Foundation, a respected philanthropically funded research body, commissioned international consultants McKinsey and Company and others to work closely with a range of energy companies across Europe to identify different energy scenarios for Europe to 2050. One of its scenarios was renewable energy scenario without nuclear power. It found that neither "nuclear nor coal-with-CCS is necessary to deliver decarbonisation while maintaining the current standard of reliability".

In a report for the Government's climate advisors, the Committee on Climate Change, consultants Poyry Management stress tested a number of detailed renewable energy scenarios using real historical weather data and 'worst case' weather data. One of these scenarios was what it called a "close to maximum" penetration of renewable energy with no new nuclear power. It found that this scenario, which was 94 per cent renewable energy, was technically feasible; with back-up gas-fired stations for times when the wind doesn't blow or sun shine. The analysis also suggested that by 2050, even with these gas-fired back-up stations, this scenario would produce only 26g [grams] of carbon per KW hour (g/KWh) of electricity demand, compared to over 440g/KWh presently. And that this figure could be reduced further through the use of hydrogen in the back-up plant rather than natural gas, and by having an optimised mix of renewable energy power plants. . . .

Nuclear Power Is Expensive

The Government claims that new nuclear power is cheaper than gas, coal or wind, at £74/MWhr [megawatts per hour]. But the reality is that new nuclear plants are far more expensive than projected. For example, construction costs have spiralled at the reactors currently being built at Flamanville in France and Olkiluoto in Finland, and both projects are years late.

The Imperial College Centre for Energy Policy and Technology (ICEPT) argues in an August 2012 working paper that the Government's figures do not reflect the realities of nuclear construction. They state the Government under-estimates construction times, cost escalation and financing costs, as well as over-estimating plant life and load factors. Imperial argues that the levelised costs—i.e. the costs excluding the need for company profits—may be over £164/MWh.

In its independent review of nuclear evidence for Friends of the Earth, the Tyndall Centre suggested that higher estimates of the cost of nuclear power are more plausible than estimates of low costs, stating that "claims that nuclear power is cheaper than other low carbon options (including CCS and wind) are unlikely to be borne out in reality".

Accountants KPMG have concluded that nuclear new build is a high risk construction project with a tendency for significant delay, cost growth and investor risk. Nuclear plants also carry high technical and regulatory risks, with World Nuclear Association figures showing very significant cost overruns for most projects, implying that utilities will only be able to pay for new plants if governments guarantee their incomes.

The Chief Executive of General Electric, one of the largest suppliers of atomic equipment, told the *Financial Times* that nuclear power is now so expensive compared with other forms of power that it is "really hard" to justify.

Nuclear Power Is Not the Answer to Climate Change

Nuclear power's latest failure to thrive despite the most lavish and ever-increasing taxpayer support is actually an unequivocal blessing. For four decades we have known that modern energy systems could threaten civilization in two ways—climate change and nuclear proliferation—so we must reject both fates, not trade one for the other. Yet new nuclear build worsens both problems. It provides do-it-yourself bomb kits in civilian disguise. It reduces and retards climate protection by saving 2–10 times less carbon per dollar—and 20–40 times more slowly—than the superior low- and no-carbon competitors that are soundly beating it in the global marketplace. But taking economics seriously and buying those cheaper options instead can protect climate, peace, and profits.

Since new nuclear build is uneconomic and unnecessary, we needn't debate whether it's also proliferative and dangerous. In a world of fallible and malicious people and imperfect institutions, it's actually both.

Amory B. Lovins, World Watch Institute, April 2011.

Direct Subsidies

Nuclear power plants are likely to operate 40 years and will require a guaranteed price for the electricity they produce for a substantial period of that operation to reduce the economic risk from building a plant that is "an order of magnitude higher in terms of costs [and] complexity" than the [2012] Olympic Stadium, which was itself described as the biggest construction project in Europe.

The government aims to provide the certainty needed by guaranteeing a set price—a so-called strike price—for a number of years through a contract called a Contract for Difference. This price will be above the market price for electricity requiring energy consumers to pay the difference and the contract may last for decades. This price is expected to be around £100/MWh and be guaranteed for 30 years or more.

By comparison, offshore wind is currently around £140/MWh, and a study by the Crown Estate has said this could be driven down to £100/MWh by 2020 with further reductions after that date. Onshore wind is already well under £100/MWh and falling.

Recent spectacular falls in solar prices have seen UK costs fall below £120/MWh for larger solar installations, and they will fall further according to McKinsey and Company who say that *"the cost of a typical commercial [roof-top] system could fall 40 percent by 2015 and an additional 30 percent by 2020"*. They also said *"The pace of cost reductions has been staggering. When companies are building new energy infrastructure, solar will be a competitive option within this decade. It will be cost comparable to peaking plant within two to three years in some countries and comparable with base load plants by the end of the decade"*.

Nuclear is a bad bet on cost grounds compared with these renewable technologies, which are likely to be much cheaper in 10–15 years. Nuclear power will be an economic millstone around the UK's neck. The Government should prioritise quicker-to-build renewable energy.

Hidden Subsidies

The economic case for nuclear is in reality even worse than this. Nuclear gets three major hidden subsidies:

• The industry gets a major subsidy by only having to insure itself very partially against a major accident

Operators get a huge public subsidy by having very limited liability in the case of accidents—at present this is 169 million Euro but may rise to a maximum of 1.2 billion Euros. This is tiny compared with potential costs—the Fukushima catastrophe cost $100–250 billion. Other industries take on far greater liabilities—for example BP put $41 billion aside for the 2011 Deepwater Horizon disaster. By not having to insure itself properly, the industry is getting a huge public subsidy. If they had to insure themselves the cost of their electricity would rise by at least £40 per MWhr.

• Operators don't pay the full cost of waste management

They are only required to pay very small sums, with limited liability, for future decommissioning costs and waste disposal costs. The use of discount rates in the economic calculations means that any cost 50+ years into the future is ignored, despite the fact that the waste will need managing for thousands of years. In addition it is highly likely that the Government has underestimated these costs. Decommissioning and waste costs are historically major underestimates—for example, the Nuclear Decommissioning Authority estimate of total decommissioning costs have risen from £47.9 billion, estimated in 2002, to a current estimate of £103.9 billion. Two-thirds of the Dept of Energy and Climate Change's budget goes on dealing with this legacy.

• Too big to fail and too big to fund

The Government has continually had to bail out the nuclear industry. Because of the risky nature of the business and the dangerous waste it generates the nuclear industry knows the Government will have to come to the rescue. It is very likely that because of the huge upfront costs of a nuclear power plant the loans the companies get from financiers will need guaranteeing by the Government. Not only will this unfairly reduce the costs of the loan—as renewable companies won't get the same guarantees—it also increases the risks to UK tax-payers.

Nuclear Power Costs Are Too Great

The Government claims that nuclear power costs £74/MWhr yet true costs are likely to be much higher, and the industry will need major subsidy through a 'Contracts for Difference'. By contrast many renewable technologies are already cheaper, and will likely fall in future, which can't be said with any confidence for nuclear. In addition, if nuclear companies had to include insurance costs for the full costs of accidents and pay full waste costs then the cost would be even higher. Opting for nuclear power is an unnecessary cost burden on energy consumers. . . .

Safety

Nuclear power has led to costly accidents which dwarf the scale of other forms of generation. Although in terms of health impacts, the Tyndall Review suggests the health impacts of coal are worse than nuclear power and states that recent life-cycle research also suggests this is the case for gas, including gas with CCS [Carbon Capture and Storage].

The Tyndall Review also suggests that currently life-cycle health impacts for renewables are broadly comparable to nuclear, but cautions that the life-cycle assessments have not accounted for all the health impacts resulting from nuclear accidents (e.g. mental health impacts as a result of relocation). There is unfortunately a paucity of quality life-cycle assessments that fully compare health impacts between the different low carbon energy supply options.

In terms of economic impact from accidents:

• The Chernobyl disaster [1986 nuclear accident in Ukraine] led to the evacuation of over 330,000 people and the creation of an exclusion zone the size of Oxfordshire. Its cost ran into hundreds of billions of dollars.

• More recently, the Fukushima accident led to the evacuation of 150,000 people from a zone 20km around the plant.

A report for the Japanese Parliament has concluded Fukushima was a "profoundly man-made disaster" citing evidence of complacency and collusion between regulators and industry. The clean-up could cost up to $250 billion.

New designs of plants are said to be much safer than both of these. Proponents say that theoretically they have probably a one-in-a million-year chance of a dangerous core damage incident per reactor and that they are also designed to withstand the impact of a Boeing 747. To date the safety record is much worse, with dangerous core damage incidence of 1 in a thousand years. Proponents also say that nuclear plants are designed to withstand earthquakes and flooding. The UK Institute of Mechanical Engineers has said that "Nuclear sites, based on the coastline, need considerable investment to protect them against rising sea levels, or even abandonment or relocation in the long term". The Tyndall Review suggested that "Climate change does not appear to present a severe risk to the safety of reactors on the UK's coasts. However, in the long-term, changes to sea level, erosion rates and storm surges may have implications for site stability, particularly during decommissioning phases. More research in this area is required." It is likely that adapting nuclear power to climate change will entail increased expense for construction, operation, waste storage and decommissioning.

However there are other issues that are not easy to eliminate, including: cyber attacks, terrorist-inspired insider sabotage and as the Japanese accident demonstrated, human error.

Even with new nuclear power designs there remains a risk, even if it is extremely small, of a catastrophic accident forcing the evacuation of tens of thousands of people, costing hundreds of billions of pounds and having significant impacts on people's mental well-being. Given that currently there are other ways to produce the energy we need and cut carbon emissions quickly Friends of the Earth believes it is a risk not worth taking.

Nuclear Waste

Nuclear power produces radioactive waste that is dangerous for tens of thousands of years. Tackling Britain's existing waste problem is expected to cost £103.9 billion. Even though new reactors will produce less waste per unit of electricity produced than older reactors, they will still add to the problem. The Tyndall Centre report stated that nuclear waste management remains an "unresolved issue" in the UK with no safe repository in place. Although a new build nuclear programme would not add significantly to the quantity of waste [it] could increase the overall radioactivity of the waste inventory by around 265 per cent.

The Royal Commission on Environmental Pollution said that "*there should be no commitment to a large programme of nuclear fission power until it has been demonstrated beyond reasonable doubt that a method exists to ensure the safe containment of long-lived, highly radioactive waste for the indefinite future*". This recommendation has been ignored.

Six years ago [in 2007], the Committee on Radioactive Waste Management (CoRWM) recommended that waste be buried deep underground at a suitable location where the local community was willing to take it. The Government accepted this recommendation but has yet to identify a suitable site. Even if a site is found it may not be ready to accept existing high level waste till 2075 and the waste from new reactors before 2130.

Britain remains decades away from having a solution for the waste we have already created. It may never to do so. To create more waste through building new nuclear plant is a folly, unless nuclear power is critical to meeting carbon dioxide reduction requirements which, as discussed above, [it is] not.

The Tyndall Centre review stated that "The proliferation risk of a new build nuclear programme in the UK is considered low in the literature. This is because the UK already has a nuclear weapons arsenal, and the 'once through' fuel cycle expected for new build does not produce material that can be easily used by other nations or organisations to develop an effective nuclear bomb". It did not consider "the political legitimacy that civilian nuclear programmes may lend to weapons programmes now or in the future" although with 65 plants under construction across the world, 167 planned, and 317 proposed, the impact of 8 plants in the UK on legitimacy should not be over-stated.

A Climate-Change Tipping Point

All the evidence is that we are facing a planetary emergency, especially with rapidly rising greenhouse gases and warnings from scientists of the potential breaching of tipping points that could lead to runaway climate change. This isn't a reason to panic but it is a reason to take a hard-headed approach in assessing technologies and practices. It also requires an ability to think out of the box and imagine a different future; or as Friends of the Earth's strap-line says, see things differently.

It was with this hard-headed, seeing things differently, approach that Friends of the Earth has reviewed the evidence for and against new nuclear power stations in the UK, aided by the Tyndall Centre at Manchester University. The review could have thrown up information or evidence that would require us to change our long-standing opposition to new nuclear power, but we undertook this review because we consider, objectively and without prejudice, the facts on the issues we work on. This is an important guiding principle given the planetary emergency context we are operating in. After receiving the Tyndall Report, and after considering it properly, we are of the view that continued opposition to new nuclear power stations in the UK is still the right position.

Britain does not need new nuclear power to meet its power needs, meet carbon reduction and electricity decarbonisation targets, or keep the lights on. Conventional nuclear power is expensive and will remain so in the future whereas the cost of renewable energy is plummeting and will do so for some time to come. It brings unique risks not faced with other energy technologies, particularly with regards to waste. The Government should abandon its fanciful plans for new conventional nuclear power.

The Government should back clean British Energy based on renewable power and energy saving. It should invest in research for newer forms of energy generation, such as deep-water off-shore wind and wave. Friends of the Earth also supports research into newer forms of nuclear power such as molten-salt thorium reactors in case of the unlikely event that they may be needed in future decades. Energy storage should be a high priority for Government funding.

> *"Power plants can still dump unlimited amounts of carbon pollution into the air for free. That's not right, that's not safe, and it needs to stop."*

Reducing Carbon Emissions Will Slow Climate Change

Barack Obama

Barack Obama is the forty-fourth president of the United States. In the following viewpoint, he declares that reducing carbon emissions is essential for slowing the warming effects of climate change and protecting the planet from devastation. He outlines his plan for reducing carbon emissions in the United States by enacting and enforcing strict regulation and reduction in carbon emissions produced by industry, increasing the use of clean energy, and by cutting energy waste and increasing energy efficiency. He explains that while the United States will still need to rely on oil and natural gas to meet its energy needs, at least in part, for some time to come, this fuel is increasingly coming from US sources and is thereby supplying jobs and commerce. Furthermore, he adds, natural gas reduces carbon emissions and is part of a larger, all-inclusive energy plan that incorporates renewable energy and traditional energy sources that will help to

Barack Obama, "Remarks by the President on Climate Change, Georgetown University, Washington, DC," June 25, 2013.

keep the economy moving while the United States transitions into an increasingly more sustainable energy profile. The United States is lowering its carbon emissions, he explains, but emissions are increasing in developing countries around the world. The United States must lead and support these countries in containing their emissions for the global good, he concludes, and American citizens must also voice their support for reducing carbon emissions and increasing green energy use in order to generate the political will to act in time to save the planet and preserve it for future generations.

As you read, consider the following questions:

1. Who were the first humans to orbit the moon, according to Obama?

2. What percentage of America's carbon pollution does the author say comes from power plants?

3. Where does Obama say that 75 percent of US wind energy is generated?

On Christmas Eve, 1968, the astronauts of Apollo 8 did a live broadcast from lunar orbit. So Frank Borman, Jim Lovell, William Anders—the first humans to orbit the moon—described what they saw, and they read Scripture from the Book of Genesis to the rest of us back here. And later that night, they took a photo that would change the way we see and think about our world.

It was an image of Earth—beautiful; breathtaking; a glowing marble of blue oceans, and green forests, and brown mountains brushed with white clouds, rising over the surface of the moon.

And while the sight of our planet from space might seem routine today, imagine what it looked like to those of us seeing our home, our planet, for the first time. Imagine what it looked like to children like me. Even the astronauts were amazed. "It makes you realize," Lovell would say, "just what you have back there on Earth."

And around the same time we began exploring space, scientists were studying changes taking place in the Earth's atmosphere. Now, scientists had known since the 1800s that greenhouse gases like carbon dioxide trap heat, and that burning fossil fuels release those gases into the air. That wasn't news. But in the late 1950s, the National Weather Service began measuring the levels of carbon dioxide in our atmosphere, with the worry that rising levels might someday disrupt the fragile balance that makes our planet so hospitable. And what they've found, year after year, is that the levels of carbon pollution in our atmosphere have increased dramatically.

That science, accumulated and reviewed over decades, tells us that our planet is changing in ways that will have profound impacts on all of humankind.

Curbing Climate Change

The 12 warmest years in recorded history have all come in the last 15 years. Last year [2012], temperatures in some areas of the ocean reached record highs, and ice in the Arctic shrank to its smallest size on record—faster than most models had predicted it would. These are facts.

Now, we know that no single weather event is caused solely by climate change. Droughts and fires and floods, they go back to ancient times. But we also know that in a world that's warmer than it used to be, all weather events are affected by a warming planet. The fact that sea levels in New York, in New York Harbor, are now a foot higher than a century ago—that didn't cause Hurricane Sandy, but it certainly contributed to the destruction that left large parts of our mightiest city dark and underwater.

The potential impacts go beyond rising sea levels. Here at home, 2012 was the warmest year in our history. Midwest farms were parched by the worst drought since the Dust Bowl, and then drenched by the wettest spring on record. Western wildfires scorched an area larger than the state of Maryland. Just last week [in June 2013], a heat wave in Alaska shot temperatures into the 90s.

And we know that the costs of these events can be measured in lost lives and lost livelihoods, lost homes, lost businesses, hundreds of billions of dollars in emergency services and disaster relief. In fact, those who are already feeling the effects of climate change don't have time to deny it—they're busy dealing with it. Firefighters are braving longer wildfire seasons, and states and federal governments have to figure out how to budget for that. I had to sit in on a meeting with the Department of Interior and Agriculture and some of the rest of my team just to figure out how we're going to pay for more and more expensive fire seasons.

Farmers see crops wilted one year, washed away the next; and the higher food prices get passed on to you, the American consumer. Mountain communities worry about what smaller snowpacks will mean for tourism—and then, families at the bottom of the mountains wonder what it will mean for their drinking water. Americans across the country are already paying the price of inaction in insurance premiums, state and local taxes, and the costs of rebuilding and disaster relief.

So the question is not whether we need to act. The overwhelming judgment of science—of chemistry and physics and millions of measurements—has put all that to rest. Ninety-seven percent of scientists, including, by the way, some who originally disputed the data, have now put that to rest. They've acknowledged the planet is warming and human activity is contributing to it.

So the question now is whether we will have the courage to act before it's too late. And how we answer will have a profound impact on the world that we leave behind not just to you, but to your children and to your grandchildren.

As a President, as a father, and as an American, I'm here to say we need to act.

A Good Energy Plan Is a Start

I refuse to condemn your generation and future generations to a planet that's beyond fixing. And that's why, today, I'm announcing a new national climate action plan, and I'm here to enlist your generation's help in keeping the United States of America a leader—a global leader—in the fight against climate change.

This plan builds on progress that we've already made. Last year, . . . my administration pledged to reduce America's greenhouse gas emissions by about 17 percent from their 2005 levels by the end of this decade. And we rolled up our sleeves and we got to work. We doubled the electricity we generated from wind and the sun. We doubled the mileage our cars will get on a gallon of gas by the middle of the next decade.

Here at Georgetown [University], I unveiled my strategy for a secure energy future. And thanks to the ingenuity of our businesses, we're starting to produce much more of our own energy. We're building the first nuclear power plants in more than three decades—in Georgia and South Carolina. For the first time in 18 years, America is poised to produce more of our own oil than we buy from other nations. And today, we produce more natural gas than anybody else. So we're producing energy. And these advances have grown our economy, they've created new jobs, they can't be shipped overseas—and, by the way, they've also helped drive our carbon pollution to its lowest levels in nearly 20 years. Since 2006, no country on Earth has reduced its total carbon pollution by as much as the United States of America.

So it's a good start. But the reason we're all here in the heat today is because we know we've got more to do.

In my State of the Union address, I urged Congress to come up with a bipartisan, market-based solution to climate change, like the one that Republican and Democratic senators worked on together a few years ago. And I still want to see that happen. I'm willing to work with anyone to make that happen.

But this is a challenge that does not pause for partisan gridlock. It demands our attention now. And this is my plan to meet it—a plan to cut carbon pollution; a plan to protect our country from the impacts of climate change; and a plan to lead the world in a coordinated assault on a changing climate.

This plan begins with cutting carbon pollution by changing the way we use energy—using less dirty energy, using more clean energy, wasting less energy throughout our economy.

The Clean Air Act and EPA Standards

Forty-three years ago, Congress passed a law called the Clean Air Act of 1970. It was a good law. The reasoning behind it was simple: New technology can protect our health by protecting the air we breathe from harmful pollution. And that law passed the Senate unanimously. Think about that—it passed the Senate unanimously. It passed the House of Representatives 375 to 1. I don't know who the one guy was—I haven't looked that up. You can barely get that many votes to name a post office these days.

It was signed into law by a Republican President. It was later strengthened by another Republican President. This used to be a bipartisan issue.

Six years ago [2007], the Supreme Court ruled that greenhouse gases are pollutants covered by that same Clean Air Act. And they required the Environmental Protection Agency, the EPA, to determine whether they're a threat to our health and welfare. In 2009, the EPA determined that they are a threat to both our health and our welfare in many different ways— from dirtier air to more common heat waves—and, therefore, subject to regulation.

Today, about 40 percent of America's carbon pollution comes from our power plants. But here's the thing: Right now, there are no federal limits to the amount of carbon pollution that those plants can pump into our air. None. Zero. We limit the amount of toxic chemicals like mercury and sulfur and arsenic in our air or our water, but power plants can still dump unlimited amounts of carbon pollution into the air for free. That's not right, that's not safe, and it needs to stop.

So today, for the sake of our children, and the health and safety of all Americans, I'm directing the Environmental Protection Agency to put an end to the limitless dumping of carbon pollution from our power plants, and complete new pollution standards for both new and existing power plants.

I'm also directing the EPA to develop these standards in an open and transparent way, to provide flexibility to different states with different needs, and build on the leadership that many states, and cities, and companies have already shown. In fact, many power companies have already begun modernizing their plants, and creating new jobs in the process. Others have shifted to burning cleaner natural gas instead of dirtier fuel sources.

Nearly a dozen states have already implemented or are implementing their own market-based programs to reduce carbon pollution. More than 25 have set energy efficiency targets. More than 35 have set renewable energy targets. Over 1,000 mayors have signed agreements to cut carbon pollution. So the idea of setting higher pollution standards for our power plants is not new. It's just time for Washington to catch up with the rest of the country. And that's what we intend to do. . . .

An All-of-the-Above Energy Strategy

A low-carbon, clean energy economy can be an engine of growth for decades to come. And I want America to build that engine. I want America to build that future—right here in the United States of America. That's our task.

Now, one thing I want to make sure everybody understands—this does not mean that we're going to suddenly stop producing fossil fuels. Our economy wouldn't run very well if it did. And transitioning to a clean energy economy takes time. But when the doomsayers trot out the old warnings that these ambitions will somehow hurt our energy supply, just remind them that America produced more oil than we have in 15 years. What is true is that we can't just drill our way out of the energy and climate challenge that we face. That's not possible.

I put forward in the past an all-of-the-above energy strategy, but our energy strategy must be about more than just producing more oil. . . .

Now, even as we're producing more domestic oil, we're also producing more cleaner-burning natural gas than any other country on Earth. And, again, sometimes there are disputes about natural gas, but let me say this: We should strengthen our position as the top natural gas producer because, in the medium term at least, it not only can provide safe, cheap power, but it can also help reduce our carbon emissions.

Federally supported technology has helped our businesses drill more effectively and extract more gas. And now, we'll keep working with the industry to make drilling safer and cleaner, to make sure that we're not seeing methane emissions, and to put people to work modernizing our natural gas infrastructure so that we can power more homes and businesses with cleaner energy.

The bottom line is natural gas is creating jobs. It's lowering many families' heat and power bills. And it's the transition fuel that can power our economy with less carbon pollution even as our businesses work to develop and then deploy more of the technology required for the even cleaner energy economy of the future.

Increasing Clean Energy Use

And that brings me to the second way that we're going to reduce carbon pollution—by using more clean energy. Over the past four years, we've doubled the electricity that we generate from zero-carbon wind and solar power. And that means jobs—jobs manufacturing the wind turbines that now generate enough electricity to power nearly 15 million homes; jobs installing the solar panels that now generate more than four times the power at less cost than just a few years ago.

I know some Republicans in Washington dismiss these jobs, but those who do need to call home—because 75 percent of all wind energy in this country is generated in Republican districts. And that may explain why last year, Republican governors in Kansas and Oklahoma and Iowa—Iowa, by the way, a state that harnesses almost 25 percent of its electricity from the wind—helped us in the fight to extend tax credits for wind energy manufacturers and producers. Tens of thousands of good jobs were on the line, and those jobs were worth the fight.

And countries like China and Germany are going all in in the race for clean energy. I believe Americans build things better than anybody else. I want America to win that race, but we can't win it if we're not in it.

So the plan I'm announcing today will help us double again our energy from wind and sun. Today, I'm directing the Interior Department to green light enough private, renewable energy capacity on public lands to power more than 6 million homes by 2020.

The Department of Defense—the biggest energy consumer in America—will install 3 gigawatts of renewable power on its bases, generating about the same amount of electricity each year as you'd get from burning 3 million tons of coal.

And because billions of your tax dollars continue to still subsidize some of the most profitable corporations in the history of the world, my budget once again calls for Congress to end the tax breaks for big oil companies, and invest in the clean-energy companies that will fuel our future.

Increasing Energy Efficiency

Now, the third way to reduce carbon pollution is to waste less energy—in our cars, our homes, our businesses. The fuel standards we set over the past few years mean that by the middle of the next decade, the cars and trucks we buy will go twice as far on a gallon of gas. That means you'll have to fill up half as often; we'll all reduce carbon pollution. And we built on that success by setting the first-ever standards for heavy-duty trucks and buses and vans. And in the coming months, we'll partner with truck makers to do it again for the next generation of vehicles. . . .

So using less dirty energy, transitioning to cleaner sources of energy, wasting less energy through our economy is where we need to go. And this plan will get us there faster. But I want to be honest—this will not get us there overnight. The hard truth is carbon pollution has built up in our atmosphere for decades now. And even if we Americans do our part, the planet will slowly keep warming for some time to come. The seas will slowly keep rising and storms will get more severe, based on the science. It's like tapping the brakes of a car before you come to a complete stop and then can shift into reverse. It's going to take time for carbon emissions to stabilize.

So in the meantime, we're going to need to get prepared. And that's why this plan will also protect critical sectors of our economy and prepare the United States for the impacts of climate change that we cannot avoid. States and cities across the country are already taking it upon themselves to get ready.

Miami Beach is hardening its water supply against seeping saltwater. We're partnering with the state of Florida to restore Florida's natural clean water delivery system—the Everglades. . . .

Reducing Global Carbon Emissions

Though all America's carbon pollution fell last year, global carbon pollution rose to a record high. That's a problem. Developing countries are using more and more energy, and tens of millions of people entering a global middle class naturally want to buy cars and air-conditioners of their own, just like us. Can't blame them for that. And when you have conversations with poor countries, they'll say, well, you went through these stages of development—why can't we?

But what we also have to recognize is these same countries are also more vulnerable to the effects of climate change than we are. They don't just have as much to lose, they probably have more to lose.

Developing nations with some of the fastest-rising levels of carbon pollution are going to have to take action to meet this challenge alongside us. They're watching what we do, but we've got to make sure that they're stepping up to the plate as well. We compete for business with them, but we also share a planet. And we have to all shoulder the responsibility for keeping the planet habitable, or we're going to suffer the consequences—together.

So to help more countries transitioning to cleaner sources of energy and to help them do it faster, we're going to partner with our private sector to apply private sector technological know-how in countries that transition to natural gas. We've mobilized billions of dollars in private capital for clean energy projects around the world.

Today, I'm calling for an end of public financing for new coal plants overseas—unless they deploy carbon-capture technologies, or there's no other viable way for the poorest countries to generate electricity. And I urge other countries to join this effort.

And I'm directing my administration to launch negotiations toward global free trade in environmental goods and services, including clean energy technology, to help more countries skip past the dirty phase of development and join a global low-carbon economy. They don't have to repeat all the same mistakes that we made. . . .

Citizens Must Be Involved

Understand this is not just a job for politicians. So I'm going to need all of you to educate your classmates, your colleagues, your parents, your friends. Tell them what's at stake. Speak up at town halls, church groups, PTA meetings. Push back on misinformation. Speak up for the facts. Broaden the circle of those who are willing to stand up for our future.

Convince those in power to reduce our carbon pollution. Push your own communities to adopt smarter practices. Invest. Divest. Remind folks there's no contradiction between a sound environment and strong economic growth. And remind everyone who represents you at every level of government that sheltering future generations against the ravages of climate change is a prerequisite for your vote. Make yourself heard on this issue.

I understand the politics will be tough. The challenge we must accept will not reward us with a clear moment of victory. There's no gathering army to defeat. There's no peace treaty to sign. When President [John F.] Kennedy said we'd go to the moon within the decade, we knew we'd build a spaceship and we'd meet the goal. Our progress here will be measured differently—in crises averted, in a planet preserved. But can we imagine a more worthy goal? For while we may not live to see the full realization of our ambition, we will have the satisfaction of knowing that the world we leave to our children will be better off for what we did.

"It makes you realize," that astronaut said all those years ago, "just what you have back there on Earth." And that image in the photograph, that bright blue ball rising over the moon's surface, containing everything we hold dear—the laughter of children, a quiet sunset, all the hopes and dreams of posterity—that's what's at stake. That's what we're fighting for. And if we remember that, I'm absolutely sure we'll succeed.

| "Climate sensitivity to CO_2 is much
| lower than [IPCC] models assume."

Carbon Emissions Have No Significant Impact on Climate Change

Nongovernmental International Panel on Climate Change

The Nongovernmental International Panel on Climate Change (NIPCC) comprises scientists and other experts focused upon evaluating the current science surrounding the causes and effects of climate change. In the following viewpoint, the authors reject the conclusion of the Intergovernmental Panel on Climate Change (IPCC) that levels of carbon dioxide (CO_2) and other greenhouse gases are rising because of human activity and that this is largely responsible for global warming. The NIPCC contends that, on the contrary, there is no correlation between CO_2 levels and global temperatures, and that in fact the planet has been cooling for some time, rather than warming. The author points out what it views as flaws in the IPCC's approach to the available data, maintaining that the IPCC ignored or misinterpreted several key facts largely out of a desire to force the data to support the conclusions at which it had arrived prior to conducting the study.

Nongovernmental International Panel on Climate Change, *Climate Change Reconsidered II: Physical Science 2013 Report of the Nongovernmental International Panel*, The Heartland Institute, 2013, pp. 2–3, 6–7, 9–11, 15–16. Copyright © 2013 by The Heartland Institute. All rights reserved. Reproduced by permission.

As you read, consider the following questions:

1. What is the purpose of a Red Team, according to the NIPCC?

2. What is the precautionary principle, according to the author?

3. According to the NIPCC, during what decade was the parallelism between fluctuations in ancient atmospheric temperature and CO_2 levels discovered in polar ice core samples?

Many scientists, policymakers, and engaged citizens have become concerned over the possibility that man-made greenhouse gas emissions, in particular carbon dioxide (CO_2), may be causing dangerous climate change. A primary reason for this public alarm is a series of reports issued by the United Nations' Intergovernmental Panel on Climate Change (IPCC). The IPCC claims to know, apparently with rising certainty over time, that "most of the observed increase in global average temperatures since the mid-20th century is very likely due to the observed increase in anthropogenic [human-generated] greenhouse gas concentrations". This [viewpoint] summarizes and interprets a major scientific report that refutes this claim.

The Red Team Reports

A technique frequently used in industry, government, and law when dealing with complex or controversial matters is to deploy competing Green and Red Teams to pursue alternative approaches. A Red Team provides a kind of "defense counsel" to verify and counter arguments mounted by the initial Green Team (the "prosecution") as well as discover and present alternatives the Green Team may have overlooked.

For many years, one team has dominated the global debate over climate change, the Green Team of the United Nations' Intergovernmental Panel on Climate Change (IPCC). In 2003, however, at a meeting in Milan, [Italy,] a Red Team started to emerge composed of independent scientists drawn from universities and private institutions around the world. Since 2008 that team, the Nongovernmental International Panel on Climate Change (NIPCC), has been independently evaluating the impacts of rising atmospheric concentrations of CO_2 on Earth's biosphere and evaluating forecasts of future climate effects. . . .

In keeping with its Red Team mission, NIPCC authors paid special attention to contributions that were either overlooked by the IPCC or that contain data, discussion, or implications arguing against the IPCC's claim that dangerous global warming is resulting, or will result, from human-related greenhouse gas emissions. . . . Most notably, its authors say the IPCC has exaggerated the amount of warming likely to occur if the concentration of atmospheric CO_2 were to double, and such warming as occurs is likely to be modest and cause no net harm to the global environment or to human well-being. . . .

The Scientific Method

Although the IPCC's reports are voluminous and their arguments impressively persistent, it is legitimate to ask whether that makes them good science. In order to conduct an investigation, scientists must first formulate a falsifiable hypothesis to test. The hypothesis implicit in all IPCC writings, though rarely explicitly stated, is that *dangerous global warming is resulting, or will result, from human-related greenhouse gas emissions.*

In considering any such hypothesis, an alternative and *null* hypothesis must be entertained, which is the simplest hypothesis consistent with the known facts. Regarding global warming, the null hypothesis is that *currently observed changes in global climate indices and the physical environment, as well as current chances in animal and plant characteristics, are the re-*

Key Facts About Temperature Forcings and Feedbacks

In ice core samples, changes in temperature precede parallel changes in atmospheric CO_2 by several hundred years; also, temperature and CO_2 are uncoupled through lengthy portions of the historical and geological records; therefore CO_2 cannot be the primary forcing agent for most temperature changes.

The melting of permafrost or submarine gas hydrates is not likely to emit dangerous amounts of methane at current rates of warming.

Nitrous oxide (N_2O) emissions are expected to fall as CO_2 concentrations and temperatures rise, indicating it acts as a negative climate feedback.

Nongovernmental International Panel on Climate Change, 2013.

sult of natural variability. To invalidate this null hypothesis requires, at a minimum, direct evidence of human causation of specified changes that lie outside usual, natural variability. Unless and until such evidence is adduced, the null hypothesis is assumed to be correct.

In contradiction of the scientific method, the IPCC assumes its implicit hypothesis is correct and that its only duty is to collect evidence and make plausible arguments in the hypothesis's favor. One probable reason for this behavior is that the United Nations protocol under which the IPCC operates defines climate change as "a change of climate which is attributed directly or indirectly to human activity that alters the composition of the global atmosphere and which is in addition to natural climate variability observed over comparable time periods". Not surprisingly, directing attention to only the effects of human greenhouse gas emissions has resulted in the IPCC failing to provide a thorough analysis of climate change in the round.

All three of the IPCC's lines of reasoning . . . depart from proper scientific methodology. Global climate models produce meaningful results only if we assume we already know perfectly how the global climate works, and most climate scientists say we do not. Moreover, it is widely recognized that climate models are not designed to produce *predictions* of future climate but rather what-if *projections* of many alternative possible futures. Postulates, commonly defined as "something suggested or assumed as true as the basis for reasoning, discussion, or belief," can stimulate relevant observations or experiments but more often are merely assertions that are difficult or impossible to test. Observations in science are useful primarily to falsify hypotheses and cannot prove one is correct.

The Precautionary Principle

Facing such criticism of its methodology and a lack of compelling evidence of dangerous warming, the IPCC's defenders often invoke the precautionary principle. The principle states: "Where there are threats of serious or irreversible damage, lack of full scientific certainty shall not be used as a reason for postponing cost-effective measures to prevent environmental degradation". This is a sociological precept rather than a scientific one and lacks the intellectual rigor necessary for use in policy formulation.

The hypothesis of human-caused global warming comes up short not merely of "full scientific certainty" but of reasonable certainty or even plausibility. The weight of evidence now leans heavily against the theory. Invoking the precautionary principle does not lower the required threshold for evidence to be regarded as valid nor does it answer the most important questions about the causes and consequences of climate change. Scientific principles acknowledge the supremacy of experiment and observation and do not bow to instinctive feelings of alarm nor claims of a supposed scientific "consensus". The formulation of effective public environmental policy must be rooted in evidence-based science, not an over-abundance of precaution.

Contradictions about methodology and the verity of claimed facts make it difficult for unprejudiced lay persons to judge for themselves where the truth actually lies in the global warming debate. This is one of the primary reasons why politicians and commentators rely so heavily on supposedly authoritative statements issued by one side or another in the public discussion. Arguing from authority, however, is the antithesis of the scientific method. Attempting to stifle debate by appealing to authority hinders rather than helps scientific progress and understanding.

Global Climate Models

In contrast to the scientific method . . . , computer models (called Global Climate Models or GCMs) represent speculative thought experiments by modellers who often lack a detailed understanding of underlying processes. The results of GCMs are only as reliable as the data and theories "fed" into them, which scientists widely recognize as being seriously deficient. If natural climate forcings and feedback are not perfectly understood, then GCMs become little more than an exercise in curve-fitting, or changing parameters until the outcomes match the modeller's expectations. As John von Neumann is reported to have once said, "with four parameters I can fit an elephant, and with five I can make him wiggle his trunk".

The science literature is replete with admissions by leading climate modellers that forcings and feedback are not sufficiently well understood, that data are insufficient or too unreliable, and that computer power is insufficient to resolve important climate processes. Many important elements of the climate system cannot be properly simulated by the current generation of models, including atmospheric pressure, wind, clouds, temperature, precipitation, ocean currents, sea ice, and permafrost. . . .

In general, GCMs perform poorly when their projections are assessed against empirical data. Specifically, the following forecasts made by GCMs have been falsified by real-world data:

IPCC Claim #1: A doubling of atmospheric CO_2 would cause warming between 3°C and 6°C. The increase in radiative forcing produced by a doubling of atmospheric CO_2 is generally agreed to be 3.7 Wm^2 [watts]. Equating this forcing to temperature requires taking account of both positive and negative feedbacks. IPCC models incorporate a strong positive feedback from increasing water vapor but exclude negative feedbacks such as a concomitant increase in low-level clouds— hence they project a warming effect of 3°C or more.

The IPCC ignores mounting evidence that climate sensitivity to CO_2 is much lower than its models assume. Empirical tests of climate sensitivity to increasing atmospheric CO_2 indicate negative feedbacks predominate and associated warming is likely an order of magnitude less than the IPCC projects. Atmospheric methane (CH_4) levels are rising more slowly than predicted and nitrous oxide (N_2O) emissions are expected to fall as CO_2 concentrations and temperatures rise, a negative climate feedback not taken into account by the IPCC.

Other forcings and feedbacks the IPCC has failed to take into account include increases in low-level clouds in response to enhanced atmospheric water vapor, ocean emissions of dimethyl sulfide (DMS), and the presence and total cooling effect of both natural and industrial aerosols. These natural processes are likely to offset most or even all of any warming caused by rising CO_2 concentrations. . . .

IPCC Claim #2: CO_2 caused an atmospheric warming of at least 0.3°C over the past 15 years. The IPCC's authors compare the output of unforced (and incomplete) models with a dataset that represents twentieth century global temperature. Finding a greater warming trend in the dataset than in model projections, the false conclusion is then drawn that this "excess" warming must be caused by human-related greenhouse forcing. In reality, no excess warming has been demonstrated, first because this line of argument assumes models have perfect knowledge, information, and power, which they do not. And second, because a wide variety of datasets other than the global air temperature curve favored by the IPCC do not exhibit a warming trend during the second half of the twentieth century. . . .

We conclude the current generation of GCMs are unable to make accurate projections of climate even 10 years ahead, let alone the 100-year period that has been adopted by policy planners. The output of such models should therefore not be used to guide public policy formulation until they have been validated and shown to have predictive value. . . .

A Disproven Postulate

IPCC Postulate: Increases in atmospheric CO_2 precede, and then force, parallel increases in temperature. The remarkable (and at first blush, synchronous [occurring at the same time]) parallelism that exists between rhythmic fluctuations in ancient atmospheric temperature and atmospheric CO_2 levels was first detected in polar ice core samples analyzed during the 1970s. From the early 1990s onward, however, higher-resolution sampling has repeatedly shown these historic temperature changes precede the parallel changes in CO_2 by several hundred years or more. A similar relationship of temperature change leading CO_2 change (in this case by several months) also characterizes the much shorter seasonal cyclicity manifest in Hawaiian and other meteorological measurements. In such circumstances,

changing levels of CO_2 cannot be driving changes in temperature, but must either be themselves stimulated by temperature
change, or be co-varying with temperature in response to
changes in another (at this stage unknown) variable. . . .

We conclude neither the rate nor the magnitude of the reported late twentieth century surface warming (1979–2000)
lay outside normal natural variability, nor was it in any way
unusual compared to earlier episodes in Earth's climatic history. Furthermore, solar forcings of temperature change are
likely more important than is currently recognized, and evidence is lacking that a 2° C increase in temperature (of what-
ever cause) would be globally harmful. . . .

A Cautious Climate Change Policy

Few scientists deny that human activities can have an effect on
local climate or that the sum of such local effects could hypo-
thetically rise to the level of an observable global signal. The
key questions to be answered, however, are whether the human global signal is large enough to be measured and if it is,
does it represent, or is it likely to become, a dangerous change
outside the range of natural variability?

NIPCC's conclusion, drawn from its extensive review of
the scientific evidence, is that any human global climate signal
is so small as to be embedded within the background variability of the natural climate system and is not dangerous. At the
same time, global temperature change is occurring, as it always naturally does. A phase of temperature stasis or cooling
has succeeded the mild twentieth century warming. It is certain that similar natural climate changes will continue to occur.

In the face of such facts, the most prudent climate policy
is to prepare for and adapt to extreme climate events and
changes regardless of their origin. Adaptive planning for future hazardous climate events and change should be tailored
to provide responses to the known rates, magnitudes, and

risks of natural change. Once in place, these same plans will provide an adequate response to any human-caused change that may or may not emerge.

Policymakers should resist pressure from lobby groups to silence scientists who question the authority of the IPCC to claim to speak for "climate science.". . . This criticism doesn't come from a "fringe" of the climate science community: It is stated plainly and repeated in thousands of articles in the peer-reviewed literature.

The distinguished British biologist Conrad Waddington wrote in 1941,

> It is . . . important that scientists must be ready for their pet theories to turn out to be wrong. Science as a whole certainly cannot allow its judgment about facts to be distorted by ideas of what ought to be true, or what one may hope to be true.

This prescient statement merits careful examination by those who continue to assert the fashionable belief, in the face of strong empirical evidence to the contrary, that human CO_2 emissions are going to cause dangerous global warming.

Periodical and Internet Sources Bibliography

The following articles have been selected to supplement the diverse views presented in this chapter.

Laura Barron-Lopez	"Moniz: 'Technology Is Ready' for Carbon Capture," *The Hill*, November 7, 2013.
John H. Cushman Jr.	"Global Boom in Coal Plants Begs for Carbon Capture Solution," Inside Climate News, November 22, 2013. http://insideclimatenews.org.
Andrew Doughman	"Panel of Experts on Renewable Energy Decry Climate Change," *Las Vegas Sun*, July 25, 2013.
Clare Foran	"Carbon Capture: Reality or Pipe Dream?," *National Journal*, November 14, 2013.
Mark Jaffe	"Carbon Capture Aids Environment, but Feasibility a Barrier," *Denver Post*, November 24, 2013.
Guy Lane	"Nuclear Energy Isn't the Answer to Global Warming," *Independent Australia*, May 14, 2013. www.independentaustralia.net.
Stephanie Paige Ogburn	"Cutting Soot and Methane May Not Slow Climate Change," *Scientific American*, August 13, 2013.
Christopher Paine	"NRDC Response to 'Coming Full Circle in Energy, to Nuclear,' by Eduardo Porter, *New York Times*, August 21, 2013," *NRDC Switchboard* (blog), August 23, 2013. http://switchboard.nrdc.org.
Eduardo Porter	"Coming Full Circle in Energy, to Nuclear," *New York Times*, August 21, 2013.
World Wildlife Foundation	"Climate Change Milestone Demands Shift to Renewable Energy," May 3, 2013. wwf.panda.org.

OPPOSING
VIEWPOINTS®
SERIES

CHAPTER 3

Are Western Societies' Practices Bad for the Environment?

Chapter Preface

Colony Collapse Disorder, or CCD, is the term used to describe the widespread death of honeybees, 10 million of which have died in North America alone since 2007. Researchers from the University of Maryland and scientists from the US Department of Agriculture (USDA) collected pollen from crops in East Coast areas that have had the worst and most destructive cases of CCD. They fed this pollen, which contained an average of nine different pesticides and fungicides (one contained twenty-one different chemicals), to healthy bees. They found that fungicides, which were thought to be harmless to bees, actually caused bees to be three times more susceptible to infection with a parasite that is a known cause of CCD. But the results were not clear regarding whether it was a single fungicide or a complex combination of several chemicals that created the vulnerability to infection. As a result, says Jeff Nesbit in an August 7, 2013, *U.S. News & World Report* article, "USDA may need to change the way it regulates the use of such fungicides around these crops and the bee colonies that pollinate them, and change the way it advises farmers and beekeepers about the use of such fungicides."

And because the healthy bees that were studied had mostly foraged from weeds and wildflowers *outside* crop areas, researchers conclude that exposure to the chemicals used on crops is far more widespread than previously thought. This insight leads to the logical conclusion that chemicals used to kill pests could have unintended effects on bees and other helpful organisms when combined and spread around outside of crop areas. The study concluded that

> more attention must be paid to how honey bees are exposed
> to pesticides outside of the field in which they are placed.
> We detected 35 different pesticides in the sampled pollen,
> and found high fungicide loads. The insecticides esfenvaler-

ate and phosmet were at a concentration higher than their median lethal dose in at least one pollen sample. While fungicides are typically seen as fairly safe for honey bees, we found an increased probability of Nosema infection in bees that consumed pollen with a higher fungicide load. Our results highlight a need for research on sub-lethal effects of fungicides and other chemicals that bees placed in an agricultural setting are exposed to.

CCD has major ramifications for the US agricultural industry, as bee pollination is responsible either directly or indirectly for about one in every three bites of food. Blueberries and cherries, for example, are 90 percent dependent on honeybees for pollination, and almonds are entirely dependent on honeybee pollination during the time that they bloom. According to Todd Woody in *Quartz*, "Bee populations are so low in the US that it now takes 60% of the country's surviving colonies just to pollinate one California crop, almonds. And that's not just a west coast problem—California supplies 80% of the world's almonds, a market worth $4 billion."

The death of millions of bees is clearly linked to Western agricultural practices and is an example of how these practices are thought to negatively impact the global environment. In the following chapter, viewpoint authors share their opinions on whether the Western world's fracking, electronic waste, and meat production are harmful to the environment.

> "Drilling and fracking result in signifi-
> cant greenhouse gas emissions, which
> threaten the climate on which we de-
> pend."

Fracking Is Harmful to the Environment

Food and Water Watch

Food and Water Watch is a nonprofit organization that advo-
cates for policies to improve and regulate food and drinking wa-
ter quality and sustainability. In the following viewpoint, the au-
thor argues that hydraulic fracturing, or "fracking," releases
harmful chemicals into the water supply and greenhouse gases
into the atmosphere, contributing to climate change. The author
outlines the devastating effects that climate change can have on
the world's water supply and maintains that climate change
policy should be integrated with water regulation in order to
protect the planet's water resources as well as its climate.

As you read, consider the following questions:

1. What does Food and Water Watch quote the UN as saying the cause of 20 percent of increase in water scarcity
   will be?

2. According to the author, how much revenue did American Water make in 2011?

3. How many states does the author say experienced abnormally dry or drought conditions during the first quarter of 2012?

Despite the alarming water crisis the world is facing, private interests are polluting, exploiting and selling water—a resource essential for all life. A 2009 publication, sponsored by the World Bank's International Finance Corporation and several for-profit multinational companies, predicted that by 2030 global freshwater demand would exceed available supplies by 40 percent. In addition to the increasing pollution and overuse of the available freshwater supply, climate change will exacerbate water shortages worldwide. In fact, a UN-Water report said, ". . . climate change is expected to account for about 20 percent of the global increase in water scarcity."

Yet the oil and gas industry continues to contribute to climate change and the water crisis by drilling and fracking for fossil fuels and siphoning off the water in our aquifers and watersheds. Water resources need to be protected, and the public's best interest should be put before the interests of multinational corporations.

Fracking's Climate Impact

Fossil fuel emissions are the leading source of climate-altering greenhouse gases from human activity. Hydraulic fracturing, or "fracking," is a process that the oil and gas industry uses to extract natural gas and oil from shale rock formations buried deep within the Earth. On a global scale, drilling and fracking result in significant greenhouse gas emissions, which threaten the climate on which we depend.

Climate Change and Human Activity: Many greenhouse gases exist naturally in our atmosphere and are crucial for keeping the planet habitable. At these natural levels, greenhouse gases trap and absorb some energy from solar radiation within the atmosphere and emit the rest back to space. This process, called the greenhouse effect, keeps our planet warm; without it, the Earth would freeze.

However, since the time of the Industrial Revolution, human activity has increased the amount and type of greenhouse gases entering the atmosphere. The increased concentration is intensifying the greenhouse effect by making layers of greenhouse gases thicker, trapping more heat, and releasing less energy back to the atmosphere. As a result, the climate is getting hotter. In the long term, our planet cannot accommodate the current levels of greenhouse gas emissions released from human activity.

Fracking and Climate Change: Fracking requires large quantities of water mixed with sand and toxic chemicals, which are injected underground at high pressure to crack dense rock and release oil and gas. Because natural gas is a relatively clean-burning fossil fuel compared to oil and coal, it has been touted as a potential bridge fuel for addressing climate change and transitioning to a future powered by low-carbon renewable energy resources. However, recent studies have demonstrated that increased development of shale gas may actually accelerate climate change because large amounts of methane, a potent greenhouse gas that makes up more than 90 percent of shale gas, leak during fracking.

Additionally, volatile organic compounds, including benzene and toluene, are released during fracking and can mix with nitrogen oxide emissions from diesel-fueled vehicles and equipment to form ground-level ozone. These emissions contribute to the enhanced greenhouse effect and climate change.

Industry and Water: Their Profits and Our Problems

Water belongs to the public and should be protected and preserved for the public. However, the private water industry

© 2013 Jen Sorensen

treats water as a market-based product, and some companies are selling public water resources to the oil and gas industry. The commodification of water—i.e., treating water as a commodity—combined with fracking could contribute to water scarcity and climate change.

Water-for-Profit Companies Make Money Off Fracking: Shale gas development creates a potential multibillion-dollar market for water supply and treatment services, the prospect of which could be encouraging some large investor-owned water utilities to support shale gas and downplay its water risks.

For example, during 2011, American Water—the largest publicly traded water and sewer utility in the country—sold

250 million gallons of water to a dozen gas-drilling companies, making $1.6 million in revenue. It sold water at 34 distribution points in Pennsylvania, mostly through pipeline extensions from its water systems. The company gave gas drillers a major discount on the price of water compared to what households pay—a benefit shared by other large industrial water users. On average, drillers paid 45 percent less than residential customers per gallon of water.

This disparity appears to be a result from a bias in the company's rate structure that favors large water users. Pennsylvania American Water said that it charged drillers its standard commercial rate and must serve any qualified applicant that requests service within its service area. Pennsylvania American Water's natural gas drilling company customers included ALTA Operating Company, LLC; Cabot Oil & Gas Corporation; Carrizo Oil & Gas, Inc.; EOG Resources, Inc. and Rex Energy Corporation.

Water Commodification and Drought, A Bad Mix: In Pennsylvania, for example, the Susquehanna River Basin Commission (SRBC) grants permits to private companies so they can withdraw and purchase water from the Susquehanna River basin for fracking. Many permits have been granted to oil and gas companies, and in March 2012 the SRBC approved a private water company's application to withdraw millions of gallons of water to supply to drillers for fracking. A month later in April, however, the commission placed a temporary moratorium on water withdrawals in certain areas due to severe drought conditions. This is particularly noteworthy since shale gas fracking uses significantly more water than conventional natural gas production, and unsustainable water withdrawals combined with increasing drought conditions can greatly reduce water supply.

The Impact on Weather and Water

As a U.S. Geological Survey publication said, "The hydrologic cycle describes the continuous movement of water above, on, and below the surface of the Earth." Rainfall can recharge surface and groundwater sources. Heat from the sun evaporates water back into the atmosphere as a vapor that condenses into clouds before falling again to the Earth. "Climate and freshwater systems are interconnected in complex ways," the Intergovernmental Panel on Climate Change noted. "Any change in one of these systems induces a change in the other."

Unpredictable and Extreme Weather Events: Climate change is believed to affect the water cycle and cause more extreme weather events, including heat waves, floods and droughts. Also becoming more common are tropical cyclones and other severe storms. Rising ocean temperatures will lead to more rapid evaporation.

The National Oceanic and Atmospheric Administration reported that "2011 was a record-breaking year for climate extremes, as much of the United States faced historic levels of heat, precipitations, flooding and severe weather." For example, Tropical Storm Lee caused extreme flooding in states like Pennsylvania and New York. During the first quarter of 2012, wildfires ignited along the east coast from Florida to New England, and 48 states experienced abnormally dry or drought conditions.

Impacts on Water Quality and Quantity: According to a UN-Water report: "Scarcity is also a question of water quality. Freshwater bodies have a limited capacity to process the pollutant charges of the effluents from expanding urban, industrial and agricultural uses. Water quality degradation can be a major cause of water scarcity."

Climate change has a bearing on water quality and quantity. It will intensify prolonged drought conditions, decrease freshwater availability and hinder groundwater recharge. The warmer temperatures combined with increasingly extreme storm events and droughts will also lead to more water pollution. As intense rainfall hits saturated or impervious surfaces, like roads, it cannot infiltrate the ground and instead flows overland as stormwater runoff, picking up pollutants along the way. In addition, increasing temperatures melt snowpack, ice caps and glaciers. Glacial melting causes sea levels to rise, which increases saltwater intrusion in many freshwater sources, reducing the amount of drinkable freshwater.

Fracking and the commodification of water are detrimental to people and the planet. In order to help mitigate global climate change and ensure a sustainable water supply for future generations, we must ban fracking and water commodification.

Integrating Water and Climate Change Policy

Water usage decisions should not be left to a market-based mechanism. To safeguard communities from water degradation and shortages, we should implement integrative water and climate change policies aimed to: (1) significantly reduce the amount of greenhouse gases released into the atmosphere, and (2) sustainably manage and protect all water resources. If water is treated as a commodity, it cannot adequately be protected for current or future generations.

- *Governments should foster adaptive water resource management.* As described by the Center for Island Climate Change Adaptation and Policy at the University of Hawai'i, adaptive water management is shaped by policies and rules that are: "(1) forward-looking—focused on crisis avoidance as well as crisis mitigation; (2) flexible—able to adjust to changing needs and conditions; (3) integrated—able to address climate-related impacts that cut across political and geographical boundaries; and (4) iterative—utilizing a continuous loop of monitoring, feedback, and reevaluation." Being adaptive allows water management practices to be preemptive rather than reactive.

- *Water management practices should not be solely reactive.* Proactive water protection provisions should support precautionary principles.

- *All water resources should be managed under statewide commons and the public trust framework.*

- *Fracking and the commodification of common water resources must be banned.*

> "States have been regulating [oil and gas] drilling and producing operations in the U.S. for decades to protect the below- and above-ground environments."

Fracking Is Not Harmful to the Environment

Bill Freeman

Bill Freeman is a chemical and environmental engineer and member of the Consortium of Scientists, Physicians, and Engineers for the American Institute for Technology and Science Education. In the following viewpoint, Freeman contends that hydraulic fracturing, which he says that "novices" refer to as "fracking," is beneficial, because it helps the United States achieve energy independence, and it is safe for the environment because it is an inherently safe process and special precautions are taken to ensure that anything that does happen to go wrong is minimized. Special-interest groups representing the alternative energy market are attacking fracturing to slow down its growth and to add to concern about global warming caused by emissions, Freeman says, despite the fact that there is no evidence that links any environmental parameter to carbon dioxide emissions created by humans. Freeman also maintains that underwater sources of drinking water (USDWs) are in no danger of contamination from fracturing nor are any water sources on the surface. For decades, he concludes, states have regulated drilling and have been successful in protecting the environment.

As you read, consider the following questions:

1. Geoscientist David Middleton says that US crude oil and natural gas liquid production will peak at how many barrels of oil per day by 2032, according to Freeman?

2. What does the author say is the average depth of the eight largest US shale gas fields?

3. What are ancillary operations, as described by Freeman?

The Petroleum Extraction Industry (PEI) provides the fossil fuel energy that regulates the heartbeat of the United States economy. Over the past number of years, energy independence from fossil fuels has not been achievable in the United States (U.S.). This is why foreign imports are still necessary to meet our energy needs.

As a result, industry, government, and academia are investigating alternative energies. As part of this, over the past few years, the PEI has continued to develop an old technology: hydraulic fracturing (novices call this "fracking").

Hydraulic Fracturing

What is hydraulic fracturing? It is a technology used after the drilling of a new fossil fuel well that significantly improves its productivity, a treatment whereby the below-ground fossil fuel reservoir adjacent to the wellbore [drilled hole] is fractured. This provides a high permeability pathway for the hydrocarbon fluids to flow from the below-ground reservoir into the wellbore and upwards to the surface for collection and processing at the above-ground production facility. Once the fracturing treatment is completed, the newly completed well is placed on permanent production for a number of years.

Hydraulic fracturing has the potential to help the U.S. achieve energy independence, even within the foreseeable future. According to geoscientist David Middleton, "I think that it is technically possible that US crude oil and natural gas liquid production could reach 14.4 million BOPD [barrels of oil per day] by 2028 and peak at 15.7 million BOPD by 2032. If U.S. demand remained in the 18–20 million BOPD range, the United States could come very close to being self-sufficient in crude oil." Much of what Middleton states is due to the "hydraulic fracturing" of tight shale oil formations. However, natural gas reserves are also significantly being increased in the U.S. as a result of hydraulic "fracturing" and assist in achieving energy independence, as well. "The availability of large quantities of shale gas should enable the United States to consume a predominantly domestic supply of gas for many years and produce more natural gas than it consumes."

A Controversy Is Stirred

Unfortunately, there is controversy about achieving energy independence by using fossil fuels. "Introduction of such a disruptive force has invariably drawn resistance, both monetary and political, to attack the disruptive source, or its enabler, hydraulic fracturing." Resistance comes from a number of special interest groups who claim, "It threatens the profitability and continued development of other energy sources, such as wind and solar, because it is much less expensive and far more reliable."[1]

The present [Barack Obama] administration and academicians now working on alternative energies accuse the PEI of continuing to recklessly provide fossil fuels to the public and industry that contributes to a) global warming and b) the potential endangerment of underground sources of drinking water (USDWs) by drilling and fracture treating new fossil fuel wells. This accusation is being used to stop or significantly slow down the use of hydraulic fracturing.

But, I believe it is unproven that the human use of fossil fuels causes global warming. See the January 2013 AITSE [American Institute for Technology and Science Education] Newsletter article by Professor Robert (Bob) Carter from Australia. Dr. Carter states, "The current scientific reality is that the IPCC's [Intergovernmental Panel on Climate Change's] hypothesis of dangerous global warming has been repeatedly tested, and fails. Despite the expenditure of large sums of money over the last 25 years (more than $100 billion), and the great research efforts by IPCC-related and other (independent) scientists, to date no scientific study has established a certain link between changes in any significant environmental parameter and human-caused carbon dioxide emissions." Yet global warming concerns are used to justify the expensive switch from fossil fuels to alternative energies.

Hydraulic fracturing also endangers USDWs according to environmentalists, academia, the news media, and the government. Their continuing attack on this technology retards the development and production of fossil fuel energy in the U.S., and suggest it is questionable whether or not the newly created fractures in the downhole producing reservoir actually provide a pathway for fluids to flow upwards from the reservior into USDWs.

Drinking Water Is Not Harmed

Actually, the contamination of USDWs caused from the fracturing treatment is highly unlikely. Since state regulators require strict well construction requirements before fracturing is commenced, the probability of endangerment of USDW's is one in one million well fracturing treatments, if the well producing reservoir is over 2000 feet in depth from the surface. "Further, the height of any fracture created in the reservoir by treatment is limited by rock stresses, leakage of fracture fluids

Hydraulic Fracturing Allows US Energy Independence

Thanks to hydraulic fracturing America is on the brink of energy independence, it has provided the biggest driver of job growth, lowered utility bills, and positively impacted the trade deficit, yet one small, well-funded, and vocal segment of the population is opposed to it—using false scare tactics to sway public opinion.

Marita Noon, Heartland Institute, October 8, 2013.

within the target fracturing zone, and the hundreds of natural rock barriers that border the hydrocarbon producing reservoir."[2] The average depth of the eight largest shale gas fields in the U.S. is about 8500 feet, thus makes the endangerment of USDWs from hydraulic fracturing itself almost impossible.

Opponents of fracturing treatments also claim this technology may endanger surface water adjacent to the well site. This accusation is misguided because the term "hydraulic fracturing" is being misdefined. Many opponents of hydraulic fracturing lump above-ground "ancillary operations," which are sealed with cement from the below-ground petroleum reservoir (thousands of feet below ground) where treatment fluids are injected, into the definition. Ancillary operations are those above-ground operations where fracture fluids are stored and mixed before and during injection below-ground into the shale gas reservoir. Leaks and spills can occur from these above-ground operations, but they are heavily monitored by PEI operators and rarely, if ever, cause below-ground problems. Incidentally, leaks and spills from above-ground ancillary operations can also occur during drilling and producing operations where well "fracturing treatments" are not being performed. Most, if not all, states already have regulations in place to monitor above-ground ancillary operations at PEI well sites. States have been regulating drilling and producing operations in the U.S. for decades to protect the below- and above-ground environments.

Reference

1. King, George E., Apache Corporation: "Hydraulic Fracturing 101," *SPE Journal of Petroleum Engineers*, April 2012.

2. *Ibid.*

"E-waste . . . constitutes a significant global environmental and health emergency."

Electronic Waste Is a Serious Environmental and Health Hazard

Karin Lundgren

Karin Lundgren has written a variety of articles on sustainability. In the following viewpoint, she outlines the scope and implications of the global electronic waste, or e-waste, problem, illustrating that not only does the international community lack a consistent definition of e-waste but that there is little awareness of the hidden hazards of the environmental threat posed by e-waste. Due to the high volume of e-waste generated, the hazardous materials used in electronics, the poor design that makes costly technology and specialized labor necessary, the health and environmental hazards of e-waste processing, the potential for financial corruption and exploitation of vulnerable populations, and the lack of regulation, Lundgren asserts, the problem of e-waste is a global emergency. She contends that the pollution and health damage posed by e-waste threaten both present and future generations.

As you read, consider the following questions:

1. According to Lundgren, what proportion of e-waste do large household appliances represent?

2. What percentage of heavy metals found in landfills comes from electronic waste, according to the author?

3. What countries have the highest rates of e-waste recycling, according to Lundgren?

In the last two decades, the global growth in electrical and electronic equipment production and consumption has been exponential. This is largely due to increasing market penetration of products in developing countries, development of a replacement market in developed countries and a generally high product obsolescence rate, together with a decrease in prices and the growth in internet use. Today, electrical and electronic waste (hereafter referred to as e-waste) is the fastest growing waste stream (about 4 per cent growth a year). About 40 million tonnes [metric tons] of e-waste is created each year. E-waste comprises electrical appliances such as fridges, air conditioners, washing machines, microwave ovens, and fluorescent light bulbs; and electronic products such as computers and accessories, mobile phones, television sets and stereo equipment.

As environmentally responsible waste management options are highly technological and require high financial investment, there is currently a high level of transboundary, often illegal, movement of e-waste into developing countries for cheaper recycling. Transboundary movement of e-waste is primarily profit driven. Recyclers and waste brokers are taking advantage of lower recycling costs in developing economies and at the same time avoiding disposal responsibilities at home. It is estimated that up to 80 per cent of all e-waste sent for recycling in developed countries ends up in informal e-waste recycling sites in developing countries, primarily in

Africa and Asia. In receiving countries, crude and hazardous methods of recycling are used, jeopardizing people's health and the environment. This raises an equity issue of developing countries receiving a disproportionate burden of a global problem, without having the technology to deal with it. Globalization of e-waste has adverse environmental and health implications as developing countries face economic challenges and lack the infrastructure for sound hazardous waste management, including recycling, or effective regulatory frameworks for hazardous waste management.

No Standard Definition of E-waste

There is no standard definition of e-waste. The Organisation for Economic Co-operation and Development (OECD) defines e-waste as "any appliance using an electric power supply that has reached its end-of-life". The most widely accepted definition of e-waste is as per European Commission Directive 2002/96/EC: "electrical or electronic equipment, which is waste . . . including all components, subassemblies and consumables, which are part of the product at the time of discarding". The differences in definitions of what constitutes e-waste have the potential to create disparities in both the quantification of e-waste generation and the identification of e-waste flows. The lack of a precise definition of e-waste is one of the key issues that need to be addressed on an international level.

In general, large household appliances represent the largest proportion (about 50 per cent) of e-waste, followed by information and communications technology equipment (about 30 per cent) and consumer electronics (about 10 per cent). The composition of e-waste is very diverse and differs across product lines and categories. Overall, it contains more than 1000 different substances which fall into "hazardous" and "non-hazardous" categories; significantly, the toxicity of many of the chemicals in e-waste is unknown. Broadly speaking, electronic products consist of ferrous and non-ferrous metals, plastics, glass, wood and plywood, printed circuit boards, concrete and ceramics, rubber and other items. Iron and steel constitutes about 50 per cent of e-waste followed by plastics (21 per cent), non ferrous metals (13 per cent) and other constituents. Electronic products often contain several persistent, bio-accumulative and toxic substances including heavy metals such as lead, nickel, chromium and mercury, and persistent organic pollutants (POPs) such as polychlorinated biphenyls (PCBs) and brominated flame retardants. The urgency of the problem is evident: worldwide, in the decade between 1994 and 2003, about 500 million personal computers containing approximately 718,000 tonnes of lead, 1,363 tonnes of cadmium and 287 tonnes of mercury, reached their end-of-life.

Low Public Awareness of Hazards

There is generally low public awareness of the hazardous nature of e-waste and the crude waste management techniques used in developing countries. The focus on science, service and software has distracted the public, who see those employed in the consumer electronics industry as mostly "white-collar" workers.

An additional, somewhat hidden, aspect of e-waste is that the loss of scarce metals present in e-waste has to be compensated for by intensified mining activities, and it is well known that the rapid increase in demand for raw materials used in electronic products has given rise to conflicts over resources worldwide. The e-waste recycling industry could play an important role in reducing such conflict risks by lowering the pressure on primary mining sites, such as those of gold, palladium and tantalum. . . .

E-waste's Main Issues

The main issues posed by e-waste are as follows:

High volumes—High volumes are generated due to the rapid obsolescence of gadgets combined with the high demand for new technology.

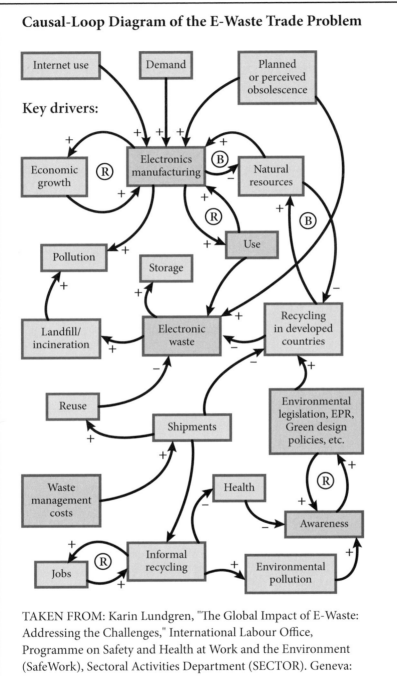

Causal-Loop Diagram of the E-Waste Trade Problem

TAKEN FROM: Karin Lundgren, "The Global Impact of E-Waste: Addressing the Challenges," International Labour Office, Programme on Safety and Health at Work and the Environment (SafeWork), Sectoral Activities Department (SECTOR). Geneva: International Labor Oganization, 2012.

Toxic design—E-waste is classified as hazardous waste having adverse health and environmental implications. Approximately 40 per cent of the heavy metals found in landfills comes from electronic waste.

Poor design and complexity—E-waste imposes many challenges on the recycling industry as it contains many different materials that are mixed, bolted, screwed, snapped, glued or soldered together. Toxic materials are attached to non-toxic materials, which makes separation of materials for reclamation difficult. Hence, responsible recycling requires intensive labour and/or sophisticated and costly technologies that safely separate materials.

Labour issues—These include occupational exposures, informal sector domination causing health and environmental problems, lack of labour standards and rights.

Financial incentives—In general, there is not enough value in most e-waste to cover the costs of managing it in a responsible way. However, in line with EPR [extended product responsibility] policies, new opportunities can be realized with the rise in the price of many of the materials in electronics, such as gold and copper. Furthermore, with rising e-waste quantities, formal recyclers are increasingly entering the e-waste recycling sector.

Lack of regulation—Many nations either lack adequate regulations applying to this relatively new waste stream, or lack effective enforcement of new e-waste regulations.

Scale of the E-waste Problem

Some of the major stakeholders in the life cycle of e-waste include producers/manufacturers, retailers (businesses/government/others), consumers (individual households/businesses/government/others), traders, exporters and importers, scrap dealers, disassemblers/dismantlers, smelters and recyclers. In developing countries, traders resell for reuse or, if equipment is unfit for reuse, often sell it to recyclers in the informal economy. Intermediaries collect functional items and sell them to repair shops. The recyclers are often special-ized in recovering specific materials. The European Union (EU) countries have the highest rates of e-waste recycling, fol-lowed by Japan. It is estimated that between 50 per cent and 80 per cent of e-waste collected for recycling in developed countries each year is being exported. Much e-waste, however, is unaccounted for. It is either discarded into the general waste stream or, perhaps, illegally exported to crude e-waste recy-cling hotspots which have been identified in Asian countries, such as China, India, and Pakistan, and in some African coun-tries, such as Ghana and Nigeria. There is a lack of informa-tion on how much e-waste is generated and where, and on where it is moving to. This situation is made worse by the current system of gathering information, in which second-hand, used and waste products are, by and large, invisible to national statistics on production, sale and trade in goods.

The demand for e-waste began to grow when scrap yards found a way of extracting valuable substances such as copper, iron, silicon, nickel and gold during the recycling process. The fast-growing economies of China and India are in need of vast amounts of materials. Domestic e-waste generation in China, Eastern Europe and Latin America is also increasing rapidly. Indeed, worldwide, all countries have increased their e-waste over time—a trend that seems unlikely to be reversed. E-waste recycling now provides employment to thousands of poor people. It is a booming, often illegal business, which fre-quently attracts migrant workers. . . .

E-waste's Effects

The degree of hazard posed to workers and the environment varies greatly depending on the individuals involved and the nature of operations. What is known is that the pollution gen-erated by e-waste processing brings about toxic or genotoxic effects on the human body, threatening the health not only of workers but also of current residents and future generations living in the local environment.

It is evident from several studies in China that the rudimentary recycling techniques coupled with the amounts of e-waste processed have already resulted in adverse environmental and human health impacts, including contaminated soil and surface water. Health problems have been reported in the last few years, including diseases and problems related to the skin, stomach, respiratory tract and other organs. Workers suffer high incidences of birth defects, infant mortality, tuberculosis, blood diseases, anomalies in the immune system, malfunctioning of the kidneys and respiratory system, lung cancer, underdevelopment of the brain in children and damage to the nervous and blood systems. However, long-term health studies of e-waste workers have yet to be conducted.

Long-range transport of pollutants has also been observed, which suggests a risk of secondary exposure in remote areas. Atmospheric pollution due to burning and dismantling activities seems to be the main cause of occupational and secondary exposure. Informal sector e-waste activities are also a crucial source of environment-to-food-chain contamination, as contaminants may accumulate in agricultural lands and be available for uptake by grazing livestock. In addition, most chemicals of concern have a slow metabolic rate in animals, and may bioaccumulate in tissues and be excreted in edible products such as eggs and milk. E-waste-related toxic effects can be exacerbated throughout a person's lifetime and across generations. E-waste therefore constitutes a significant global environmental and health emergency, with implications far broader than occupational exposure and involving vulnerable groups and generations to come.

| "*The toxic tide [of e-waste] that fright-ened Americans into stashing their old computers in closets turns out to be nothing more threatening than a trickle.*"

The Environmental and Health Effects of Electronic Waste Are Exaggerated

Adam Minter

Adam Minter is the Shanghai, China, correspondent for the Bloomberg World View *blog. In the following viewpoint, he contends that the prevailing opinion that the United States is creating a global e-waste emergency in the developing world is based on false information. Rather, he argues, a study by the US International Trade Commission finds that most of the e-waste generated in the United States remains in and is repaired, dis-mantled, or recycled in the United States. Minter contends that the misinformation has led to policies that have kept much-needed electronics out of the developing world where they could help to close the digital gap and stimulate growing economies. Most US e-waste, he explains, is sent to countries that have state-of-the-art processing facilities and very little is sent to the developing world. In addition, he asserts, recycling e-waste has created jobs in the United States.*

As you read, consider the following questions:

1. What percentage of e-waste that Americans generated in 2011 was sent overseas, according to Minter?

2. What did a 2011 United Nations study determine was the percentage of used electronics imported by Nigeria that did not work or was unrepairable, according to the author?

3. What country does Minter say has one of the world's best and cleanest factories for the extraction of precious metals from circuit boards and other devices?

E very year, Americans toss out as much as 4.5 million tons of old mobile phones, laptops, televisions, Xboxes and other electronic gadgets.

Some is recycled; some is repaired and refurbished for re-use; and some is thrown into landfills or incinerators. Almost none of it, however, is "dumped" overseas.

That, at least, is the conclusion of the first comprehensive survey of what happens to U.S. e-waste after it is dropped into a recycling bin. Published in February [2013], the study by the U.S. International Trade Commission surveyed 5,200 businesses involved in the e-waste industry (companies that received the survey were required by law to complete it, and to do so accurately), and found that almost 83 percent of what was put into American recycling bins in 2011 was repaired, dismantled or recycled domestically.

According to the same survey, only 0.13 percent of the 4.4 million tons of e-waste that Americans generated in 2011 was sent overseas for "final disposal"—a term that explicitly excludes recycling and reuse—with an additional 3 percent sent abroad for "unknown" purposes.

Reality is a far cry from the long-standing claim, first made by the Basel Action Network, a Seattle-based nongovernmental organization in 2002, that as much as 80 percent of U.S. e-waste is exported to the developing world. Amazingly, even with the wide currency the claim has enjoyed over the years among environmental organizations and the media, it was never based on a systematic study.

Misguided Efforts

This misunderstanding has led to several efforts at erecting partial export bans on U.S. electronics to developing countries, which—other studies demonstrate—import them as cheap and sustainable alternatives to new equipment. As a result, perfectly usable electronics are diverted into a recycling stream, where they are turned into raw materials, rather than into markets where they can be reused for years.

There are no statistics on how many used gadgets were exported from the U.S. to the developing world in 2002. Nor, for that matter, can anyone say for sure what happened to those gadgets. No doubt, many were broken down in developing-world facilities, where low-technology and often-hazardous methods of recycling and disposal were employed (such as the use of acids to strip copper and other metals from circuit boards in open, unprotected environments).

Anecdotally, I have been told by recyclers in southern China that cheap, secondhand electronics exported from the U.S. and, to a lesser extent, the European Union were used by Chinese computer labs, offices and dormitories in the 1990s through the mid-2000s, when new gadgetry simply wasn't affordable. (There has been no comprehensive survey to verify these claims, however.)

It was a good deal for the U.S., too: In the 1990s and early 2000s, America didn't really have an electronics-recycling sector, and those machines would have been put in a landfill if

China hadn't wanted them. Nonetheless, as China developed, and incomes rose, demand for those used machines dropped off.

The good news is that a similar cycle is occurring in Africa, where used electronics from the EU and the U.S. have become a critical means of bridging the global digital gap. Unlike Chinese imports in the 1990s and early 2000s, the African imports are being surveyed and quantified.

For example, a 2011 study by the United Nations Environment Program determined that only 9 percent of the used electronics imported by Nigeria—a country that is regularly depicted as a dumping ground for foreign e-waste—didn't work or were unrepairable, and thus bound for a recycler or a dump. The other 91 percent were reusable and bound for consumers who couldn't afford new products.

The Nigerian Experience

That certainly doesn't excuse the hazardous means that some Nigerians use to recycle old electronics (and, increasingly, those old electronics are thrown away by middle-class Nigerians, rather than being imported from abroad). Yet it also doesn't suggest that the U.S., Europe or even China (a growing source of e-waste) are to blame, either.

So what happens to the 14 percent of U.S. e-waste that isn't processed domestically, sent for "final disposal" in other countries, or isn't otherwise unknown? According to the trade commission report, most is exported as recycled commodities to be reused by manufacturers in new products; as reusable gadgets; and even as warrantied products for repair.

Less than half of those exports, by weight, go to developing countries; the majority is shipped to member countries of the Organization for Economic Co-operation and Development, such as Japan and Belgium, where the recyclable material is handled better in factories than it can be in America.

The U.S. shipped almost three times as much e-waste to Belgium in 2011 as it did to sub-Saharan Africa, according to the trade commission.

Why? Belgium has one of the world's best (and cleanest) factories for the extraction of precious metals from circuit boards and other complicated devices. It is thus capable of paying far more for them than a recycler in Nigeria with little more than some jars of acid capable of refining gold, though not platinum and other precious metals.

The biggest story embedded in the trade commission's story isn't that U.S. e-waste exports are greener than ever. Rather it is that the domestic electronics-recycling industry has grown into a large, mature business that views export as a second choice, not the first one.

The industry generated sales of $20.6 billion in 2011, compared with less than $1 billion in 2002, according to figures from the trade commission as well as the Institute of Scrap Recycling Industries, an industry association.

Recycling Jobs

E-Stewards, a strict, U.S.-based electronics recycling certification standard that bans most exports, has grown from having zero member facilities certified in 2010 to 102 in 2013, including several belonging to Waste Management, North America's largest recycling company. Most of what these companies— certified or not—produce are commodity-grade raw materials, such as metals and plastics, usable for new products in the U.S. and abroad.

More revealing, yet, is the employment picture: The institute estimates full-time jobs in the U.S. electronics-recycling industry grew to more than 45,000 in 2011 from 6,000 in 2002. Some of those employees, no doubt, are involved in packing used electronics for shipment around the world, including to places where unsafe, environmentally damaging means of disposal are still used.

Thanks to the International Trade Commission findings and other, smaller-scale studies, we now know that most secondhand electronics are reused and recycled in the U.S. The toxic tide that frightened Americans into stashing their old computers in closets turns out to be nothing more threatening than a trickle.

> *"Agriculture, through meat production, is one of the main contributors to the emission of greenhouse gases . . . and thus has a potential impact on climate change."*

Meat Production Is a Major Contributor to Climate Change

United Nations Global Environmental Alert Service

The United Nations Global Environmental Alert Service (GEAS) researches and reports on emerging issues of concern for the global environment to the United Nations Environment Programme. In the following viewpoint, the GEAS argues that livestock raised for meat consumption are a major source of greenhouse gas emissions and significantly contribute to climate change. In fact, the GEAS asserts, livestock emissions make up nearly 80 percent of emissions from agriculture, and agricultural emissions make up an estimated 10 to 35 percent of total global emissions. Methane and nitrous oxide, the author contends, are the primary greenhouse gases emitted by livestock when they digest food and produce manure. The "factory" model of agriculture, wherein animals are housed in concentrated animal feeding operations (CAFOs), the GEAS argues, has replaced the traditional model of agriculture in which animals feed from and fertilize grazing areas, and this has greatly increased emissions because of the types of chemically fertilized feed that the animals eat, the emissions generated by transporting the feed long distances, and the contamination of water from enormous amounts of manure that are generated by thousands of animals living in concentrated areas. In order to mitigate the environmental damage caused by such meat production, the GEAS concludes, the agricultural community must engage in practices like soil carbon sequestration (putting carbon dioxide into the soil rather than the atmosphere) and increased grass-feeding of cows. Humans must also change their diets, maintains the author, to include far less amounts of red meat and dairy products and far greater amounts of fruits, vegetables, and grains.

As you read, consider the following questions:

1. What percentage of the 1.43 billion cattle around the world does the GEAS say were in Asia in 2010?

2. How many miles of automobile use are represented by the consumption of one kilogram of domestic beef, according to the author?

3. How many fewer deaths per year in the UK does the author contend there would be if meat and dairy consumption were reduced by 50 percent and replaced with fruit, vegetables, and cereals?

Both intensive (industrial) and non-intensive (traditional) forms of meat production result in the release of greenhouse gases (GHGs). As meat supply and consumption increase around the world, more sustainable food systems must be encouraged.

Why Is This Issue Important?

For many thousands of years, mankind has lived in close proximity with numerous animal species, providing them with food and shelter in exchange for their domestic use and for products such as meat and milk, feathers, wool and leather. As the economy in some (mostly western) countries slowly grew, industrial style agriculture replaced traditional small-scale farming. Pasturage [letting animals graze] and use of animal manure as fertilizer was abandoned. The increasing efficiency of industrial agriculture has led to reduced prices for many of our daily products. It helped to reliably nourish large populations, and turned a food that was an occasional meal—meat—into an affordable, every-day product for many.

However, the true costs of industrial agriculture, and specifically "cheap meat", have become more and more evident. Today, [according to a UN Food and Agriculture Organization study by H. Steinfeld et al.,] "the livestock sector emerges as one of the top two or three most significant contributors to the most serious environmental problems." This includes stresses such as deforestation, desertification, "excretion of polluting nutrients, overuse of freshwater, inefficient use of energy, diverting food for use as feed and emission of GHGs." Perhaps the most worrisome impact of industrial meat production, analyzed and discussed in many scientific publications in recent years, is the role of livestock in climate change. The raising of livestock results in the emission of methane (CH_4) from enteric fermentation [the digestive process] and nitrous oxide (N_2O) from excreted nitrogen, as well as from chemical nitrogenous (N) fertilizers used to produce the feed for the many animals often packed into "landless" Concentrated Animal Feeding Operations (CAFOs). . . .

Meat Production and Climate Change

Agriculture, through meat production, is one of the main contributors to the emission of greenhouse gases (GHGs) and thus has a potential impact on climate change. Estimates of the total emissions from agriculture differ according to the system boundaries used for calculations. Most studies attribute 10–35 per cent of all global GHG emissions to agriculture. Large differences are mainly based on the exclusion or inclusion of emissions due to deforestation and land use change.

Recent estimates concerning animal agriculture's share of total global GHG emissions range mainly between 10–25 per cent, where again the higher figure includes the effects of deforestation and other land use changes and the lower one does not. . . . Emissions from livestock constitute nearly 80 per cent of all agricultural emissions.

Types of Emissions

In contrast to general trends of GHG emissions, carbon dioxide (CO_2) is only a small component of emissions in animal agriculture. The largest share of GHG emissions is from two other gases: methane (CH_4) and nitrous oxide (N_2O). These are not only emitted in large quantities, but are also potent greenhouse gases. . . .

Globally, about 9 per cent of emissions in the entire agricultural sector consist of CO_2, 35–45 per cent of methane and 45–55 per cent of nitrous oxide.

The main sources of CH_4 are the enteric fermentation of ruminants [cud-chewing mammals] and releases from stored manure, which also emits N_2O. The application of manure as well as N fertilizers to agricultural land increases emissions of N_2O. Furthermore, N_2O as well as CO_2 are released during production of chemical N fertilizers. Some CO_2 is also produced on farms from fossil fuels and energy usage and, as some authors highlight, by the exhalation of animals, which is generally not taken into account. Additionally, deforestation and conversion of grassland into agricultural land release considerable quantities of CO_2 and N_2O into the atmosphere, as the soil decomposes carbon-rich humus [material in soil from decomposed organic matter]. In Europe (the EU-27), for example, enteric fermentation was the main source (36 per cent) of GHG emissions in the livestock sector, followed by N_2O soil emissions (28 per cent). Livestock are also responsible for almost two-thirds (64 per cent) of anthropogenic [human-caused] ammonia emissions, which contribute significantly to acid rain and acidification of ecosystems.

Cattle Are the Main Culprits

Cattle are by far the largest contributors to global enteric CH_4 emissions, as they are the most numerous and have a much larger body size relative to other species such as sheep and goats. Out of the 1.43 billion cattle in 2010, 33 per cent were in Asia, 25 per cent in South America and 20 per cent in Africa. Asia is the main source of CH_4 emissions, with almost 34 per cent of global emissions. China is a major source of enteric emissions and, while Indians are low meat consumers, India as a country also has high levels of CH_4 emissions. Latin America follows with 24 per cent and Africa with 14.5 per cent. China, Western Europe and North America are the regions with the highest emissions from manure.

Emissions for a Meal

In an analysis of the EU-27 countries [by researchers J.P. Lesschen et al.], "beef had by far the highest GHG emissions. . . ." [Researchers A. Carlsson-Kanyama et al.] conclude that "it is more 'climate efficient' to produce protein from vegetable sources than from animal sources", and add that "beef is the least efficient way to produce protein, less efficient than vegetables that are not recognized for their high protein content, such as green beans or carrots". In terms of GHG emissions [Carlsson-Kanyama et al. state,] "the consumption of 1 kg domestic beef in a household represents automobile use of a distance of $\sim$ 160 km (99 miles)."

The Environmental Benefits of Pasture-Based Meat Production

Our review of the relevant literature finds general agreement among scientists that raising cattle on well-managed pastures will provide significant environmental and other benefits:

- Decreased soil erosion and increased soil fertility

- Improved water quality (due to decreased pollution)

- Improved human health (due to reduced antibiotic use)

- Improved farmer and farm worker health

- Improved animal health and welfare

- More profit per animal for producers

Kate Clancy, Union of Concerned Scientists, March 2006.

Animal Feed and Manure

Under natural conditions which were maintained for thousands of years and still widely exist around the world, there is a closed, circular system, in which some animals feed themselves from landscape types which would otherwise be of little use to humans. They thus convert energy stored in plants into food, while at the same time fertilizing the ground with their excrements. Although not an intensive form of production, this co-existence and use of marginal resources was, and still is in some regions, an efficient symbiosis between plant life, animal life and human needs.

In many parts of the world "traditional" forms of animal agriculture have to a certain extent been replaced by a "landless", high-density, industrial-style animal production system, exemplified by the phenomenon known as Concentrated Animal Feeding Operations (CAFO). Those "factories" hold hundreds or thousands of animals, and often buy and import animal feed from farmers far away. The feeding of livestock, and their resulting manure, contributes to a variety of environmental problems, including GHG emissions. High-energy feed is based on soya and maize [corn] in particular, cultivated in vast monocultures and with heavy use of fertilizers and herbicides. It is then imported (at least in Europe and most parts of Asia) from countries as far away as Argentina and Brazil. This has serious consequences in terms of land-use change in those feed-for-export production countries. Furthermore, this manure is generated in huge quantities. In the USA alone, operations which confine livestock and poultry animals generate about 500 million tonnes of manure annually, which is three times the amount of human sanitary waste produced annually. Insufficient amounts of land on which to dispose of the manure results in the runoff and leaching of waste into and the contamination of surface and groundwater.

Undermining Agriculture

Livestock in many regions of the world, and especially in dry areas, act as a "savings bank": a principal way of making use of a harsh environment, a "setting aside" of food (and more generally, the value of this resource) for dry times, a main source of high-protein food. It contributes important non-food goods and services. Livestock rearing and consumption in these regions is a way of life, critical to pastoralists' identity, and should be protected and supported.

At present, the ecological foundations of agriculture are being undermined. At the same time, industrial agriculture is itself contributing to environmental problems such as climate change. However, there are mitigation techniques to reduce the impact of both intensive and non-intensive animal production on climate. Most of these are related to soil carbon sequestration [putting carbon dioxide into soil rather than air].... Many of them have costs of implementation substantially reducing their potential. A reduction of non-carbon dioxide emissions of up to 20 per cent should, however, be possible at realistic costs. Other mitigation solutions include improved feedstock efficiency and diets; the reduction of food waste and improved manure management....

Changing the Human Diet

Changes in human diet may also be a practical tool to reduce GHG emissions. As a large percentage of beef is consumed in hamburgers or sausages, [Carlsson-Kanyama et al. note that] "the inclusion of protein extenders from plant origin would be a practical way to replace red meats." A switch to less "climate-harmful" meat may also be possible, as pigs and poultry produce significantly less methane than cows. They are however more dependent on grain and soy-products and may thus still have a negative impact on GHG emissions. Grass-fed meat and resulting dairy products may be more environmentally friendly than factory-farmed or grain-fed options. Labeling of products, indicating the type of animal feed used, could allow consumers to make more informed choices.

Scientists agree that in order to keep GHG emissions to 2000 levels the projected 9 billion inhabitants of the world (in 2050) need to each consume no more than 70–90 grams of meat per day. To meet this target, substantial reductions in meat consumption in developed countries and constrained growth in demand in developing ones would be required. A reduction in the consumption of meat, especially red meat, could have multiple health benefits, as there is clear evidence of a link between high meat diets and bowel cancer and heart disease. A study modeling consumption patterns in the United Kingdom estimates that a 50 per cent reduction in meat and dairy consumption, if replaced by fruit, vegetable and cereals, could result in a 19 per cent reduction in GHG emissions and up to nearly 43,600 fewer deaths per year in the UK. However, the health effects of nutrient deficiencies that may result from reduced meat and dairy consumption still would need to be examined.

In short, the human health implications of a reduced meat diet need further exploration, but it seems probable that many benefits would accrue from lower consumption rates in many developed and some developing countries. At the same time, reduced meat production would ease both pressures on the remaining natural environment (i.e. less new land clearance for livestock) and on atmospheric emissions of CO_2, CH_4 and N_2O. As changing the eating habits of the world's population will be difficult and slow to achieve, a long campaign must be envisioned, along with incentives to meat producers and con-sumers to change their production and dietary patterns. "Healthy" eating is not just important for the individual but for the planet as a whole.

> *"Decreasing meat and milk production will only result in more hunger in poor countries—not a cleaner or cooler environment . . ."*

Meat Production's Contribution to Climate Change Is Exaggerated

Rod Smith

Rod Smith is a contributor for Feedstuffs, *a weekly newspaper for agribusiness. In the following viewpoint, the author contends that the often-cited and widely believed reports of the damaging effects of animal agriculture are based on distorted information and a lack of understanding of the relationship between animals, humans, and the atmosphere. The author argues that livestock production is not to blame for most greenhouse gas emissions, and in fact accounts for only a fraction of the total emission in the United States. Not only is meat production environmentally safe and sustainable, according to the author, the quality of the meat has improved, and humans are living longer due to meat-rich diets. The author concludes that there are many confusing and conflicting arguments about livestock production, and it is important for people to sort through them.*

As you read, consider the following questions:

1. According to Mitloehner, why do critics fail to understand the relationship between animal and food production?

2. How much does Mitloehner say that livestock production actually contributes to greenhouse gas emissions?

3. Why do critics believe that livestock production casts a larger carbon footprint than it actually does, according to the author?

Animals need to be produced in a smarter manner—not in fewer numbers—to address environmental issues related to climate change, according to Frank Mitloehner, an associate professor and air quality specialist at the University of California-Davis.

Decreasing meat and milk production will only result in more hunger in poor countries—not a cleaner or cooler environment, he said in response to critics of meat and milk production who blame livestock for significant global warming.

Mitloehner said these critics fail to understand the relationship among animal and food production, animal digestion, human activities and atmospheric chemistry.

He traced much of this lack of understanding to two sentences in a 2006 U.N. report, "Livestock's Long Shadow," which stated that the "livestock sector is a major player, responsible for 18% of greenhouse gas emissions measured in carbon dioxide equivalents. This is higher than transport."

He said findings in the U.S. show that livestock production accounts for only 2.8% of emissions in the U.S., while transportation accounts for 26% (*Feedstuffs*, Dec. 14, 2009).

Accordingly, he said the focus should be on creating more efficient livestock production and transferring livestock production technology to developing countries where people need a more abundant and nutritious food supply.

Mitloehner will raise these points during remarks to the annual meeting of the National Meat Assn. in Indian Wells, Cal., next month.

In making similar points, the National Cattlemen's Beef Assn. recently added that the entire agriculture sector represents just 6% of total U.S. emissions and that land use, land use change and forestry activities cause net carbon sequestration of 17.4% of total U.S. carbon dioxide emissions, or 14.9% of total domestic greenhouse gas emissions.

Eating Confidently

In addition to being efficient and environmentally sustainable, the U.S. meat supply also is safe, according to the American Meat Institute (AMI), which noted that the meat industry "is the most inspected and regulated" in the U.S. and that the industry has "an excellent food safety record that reflects progress."

AMI said a number of recent news stories have questioned the safety of the meat supply—particularly the safety of the beef supply—and listed several points in response, including:

- Almost 8,000 federal food inspectors oversee 6,200 meat plants across the country. Plants that process live animals have inspectors on site during every minute of livestock processing and meat production, and large plants have as many as 24 inspectors on site who are authorized to halt production at any time and prevent meat from entering commerce.

- Since 2000, the incidence of Escherichia coli O157:H7 in ground beef has decreased 45% to less than 0.5% of production, based on U.S. Department of Agriculture sampling data.

- Since 2000, the incidence of E. coli O157:H7 infections in people has decreased 44%, according to the Centers for Disease Control & Prevention.

- Since 2000, the incidence of salmonella in ground beef has decreased more than 50%, based on USDA sampling data.

- Meat products carry federally mandated safe handling labels that offer advice for preparing the products so they are cooked thoroughly to destroy any bacteria remaining on the products and are safe to consume.

"Food safety data show that we (the meat industry) take our responsibility seriously" to produce safe and wholesome food, AMI president J. Patrick Boyle said. "We confidently feed our families the same meat products that we sell to our customers in the U.S. and around the world."

Outliving Apes

In addition to being efficiently produced, environmentally sustainable and safe, meat might well be behind the reason people live longer lives than any other primate, according to biologist Caleb Finch at the University of Southern California in Los Angeles, Cal.

Apes and chimpanzees are genetically similar to humans but rarely live more than 50 years, and it is possible that genetic changes that allow people to live longer are attributable to eating a more carnivorous diet than apes and chimps, he told the LiveScience program on TechMediaNetwork.

The human lifespan has doubled in the last 200 years due to decreased infant mortality and improvements in diets, medicine and the environment, and even in societies that are less advanced, people still live longer than apes and chimps, Finch said.

He suggested that this is related to a genetic change that has permitted people to consume meat-rich diets.

Some of the oldest stone tools ever made suggest that early humans made tools 2.6 million years ago to butcher animals, and as they evolved, they became more adapted to digesting meat, a high-energy food, Finch said.

In the era before cooking, eating meat that was infected with parasites caused chronic inflammation to which people developed unique variants in a cholesterol-transporting gene, apolipoprotein E (ApoE), that regulates not only this inflammation but many aspects of aging in the arteries and brain, he explained.

In fact, one such variant found in modern populations, ApoE3, emerged some 250,000 years ago and decreases the risk of most age-related diseases, specifically Alzheimer's disease and heart disease, Finch said.

He theorized that ApoE3 evolved to lower the risk of degenerative disease from high-fat meat diets. It also is linked to brain development and longer life, he said.

Here's the Point

Some sources came to the defense of meat recently, and not all of them are associated with the meat industry.

An air quality specialist said livestock production casts a much smaller carbon footprint than critics say because those critics—who argue that livestock and, therefore, meat production contribute to global warming—are using erroneous information and don't understand the differences between animal and human activities and atmospheric chemistry. He said decreasing livestock production would not only have no real effect on global warming but would deny hungry people the benefits of meat and milk.

In addition, a biologist said meat, which people have been consuming for more than 2 million years, has, over time, stimulated the development of genes that have decreased age-related diseases, promoted brain development and let people live longer and more productive lives.

Also, a meat industry official commented on meat safety, noting that the industry is highly inspected and has initiated important interventions and taken other steps in the last 10 years to make meat safer and more wholesome. He noted that in the last 10 years, the meat industry, based on the U.S. Department of Agriculture's own sampling, has significantly decreased the prevalence of Escherichia coli O157:H7, salmonella and other bacteria on meat.

These are important messages for people struggling to sort through conflicting and confusing arguments and claims about livestock, meat and milk production. Information on these matters and other aspects of modern U.S. agriculture can be found at www.FeedstuffsFoodLink.com.

Periodical and Internet Sources Bibliography

The following articles have been selected to supplement the diverse views presented in this chapter.

Environmental Leader	"UN: Treated Waste Could Be 'Gold Mine,'" October 10, 2013. www.environmentalleader .com.
Elliot Hannon	"Norway's Army Goes Vegetarian to Combat Climate Change," *Slate*, November 20, 2013. www.slate.com.
Curt Harler	"Trash or Treasure?," Recycling Today, April 1, 2013. www.recyclingtoday.com.
Marita Noon	"Thanks to Fracking USA Rises to Number One in Energy; Thanks to Obama, We Won't Stay There," *Somewhat Reasonable* (blog), October 8, 2013. http://blog.heartland.org.
Hannah Osborne	"China and India Driving Global Meat Consumption but West Still Worst Offender," *International Business Times*, December 3, 2013. www.ibtimes.co.uk.
Barry Poulson	"Weld County, Colorado: Ground Zero in the Anti-fracking Battle," *Forbes*, December 4, 2013.
Valerie Richardson	"Fracking Supporters Fire Back at 'Woefully Misinformed' Celebrities," *Washington Times*, December 3, 2013.
David Sirota	"The Problem with Meat Consumption Isn't Just Hyperbole," *Coloradoan* (Fort Collins, CO), December 5, 2013.
Katie Valentine	"Researchers Link Earthquakes in Texas to Fracking Process," *Climate Progress*, December 6, 2013. http://thinkprogress.org.

CHAPTER 4

What Policies Will Improve the Environment?

Chapter Preface

On October 29, 2013, the US Treasury Department released new guidelines that spell out quite clearly that President Barack Obama's administration is resolved to uphold its commitment to deny US funding for conventional coal-fired plants abroad except in "very rare" cases. This policy affects US support for new coal plants or modifications to existing coal plants that have been funded through the World Bank, which is a multilateral development bank. In order to receive US funding, new coal plants would have to include carbon capture and sequestration technology, and adhere to the same greenhouse gas emissions standards that the Environmental Protection Agency enforces for new US power plants. Essentially, all new coal plants funded by the US would need to keep emissions at the same level or lower than the emissions of a natural-gas power plant of a similar size.

Only the poorest countries could be allowed funding to build coal plants without such technology and emissions requirements, in cases in which there are no alternative sources of power and it would severely impact the country's development. Prior to the release of the new guidelines, the administration's position was one of "discouraging" US funding for coal plants without carbon capture technology, but the new guidelines reflect a commitment to helping the developing world increase its use of clean energy that Obama outlined in his Climate Action Plan during a June 2013 speech. Reporting for the news agency Reuters, Anna Yukhananov says that the "United States is the World Bank's largest and most powerful member but likely would still have to build coalitions with other countries if it wanted to block funding for a specific coal project." Yukhananov added that the "World Bank last approved funding for a coal-fired power plant in 2010 in South Africa, despite lack of support from the United States,

Netherlands and Britain due to environmental concerns." That same day, Lael Brainerd, undersecretary for international affairs at the Treasury, was quoted by Michael Shears in the *New York Times* as saying, "We believe that if public financing points the way, it will then facilitate private investment."

An embargo on coal plant funding is one policy whose supporters hope will reduce pollution and carbon emissions and thereby improve the environment. Other policies aimed at improving the environment that are debated by authors in the following chapter are bans on plastic bags and the mandated implementation of extended producer responsibility for goods produced, packaged, and sold in the United States and elsewhere.

> "When it comes to plastic bags, there's only one thing to do that's 100% effective. Ban them."

Plastic Bag Bans Protect the Environment

Stiv Wilson

Stiv Wilson is a journalist and policy director for the 5 Gyres Institute. In the following viewpoint, which he wrote in response to claims by other writers that plastic bags are not a problem, he maintains that recycling or reusing plastic does not eliminate the hazards that it poses to the environment; the only way to eliminate the hazards of plastic bags, he asserts, is to ban them. He contends that there is plastic pollution in all five major gyres, which are circular systems of currents in the world's largest oceans, but that there is no way to know precisely how much. What is known, he asserts, is that plastic bags are by far the largest source of marine pollution. And when a plastic bag is recycled, he says, it generates three new bags. The campaign to scare people away from using reusable shopping bags by claiming that they are full of bacteria, he maintains, is a hoax meant to drive up the sales of "hybrid" plastic bags. Companies that claim to be recycling plastic bags, Wilson says, are lying; the truth is that less than 1 percent of plastic bags are ever recycled.

As you read, consider the following questions:

1. Who founded the 5 Gyres Institute, according to Wilson?

2. What percentage of beach trash worldwide does Wilson say is plastic bags?

3. How much of domestic natural gas mining comes from fracking, according to the author?

Full disclosure: I'm a journalist turned activist who works for a nonprofit called the 5 Gyres Institute founded by Dr. Marcus Eriksen and Anna Cummins to research, educate and act on issues pertaining to plastic and chemical pollution in the marine environment as well as the watersheds that feed them. As 5 Gyres' Policy Director, I have worked tirelessly on chemical, plastic bottle and bag bans across the country. It is my goal to take an objective view of the facts, investigating industry and [other] claims in order to ultimately inform the positions of educators, stakeholders and policymakers.

Studying Plastic Pollution

As a surfer, I started noticing plastic everywhere on every beach in the world where I traveled about ten years ago [ca. 2001]. It bothered me. As I became more versed on the subject of maritime plastic pollution, I was invited by 5 Gyres to participate in a research voyage to the North Atlantic Gyre,[1] and after seeing what I saw out there, firsthand, over 1,000 miles from land, I quit my job at a media company and started working on plastic pollution issues full time.

Since that voyage, I've sailed across two other oceanic gyres now, the South Atlantic and the South Pacific, witnessing the same pollution in two other oceans. It is exceptionally

1. A gyre in oceanography is a large system of rotating ocean currents. The five main gyres are in the Indian Ocean, the North Atlantic, North Pacific, South Atlantic, and South Pacific Oceans.

sad and difficult to explain what plastic pollution in a gyre looks like, but when you see plastic films floating on the surface, two weeks from land under full sail, it starts to give you the cosmic heebie-geebies.

What's at issue is this:

> Plastic does not biodegrade in a meaningful if even comprehensible timeframe. Thus, some portion of it accumulates in the environment. The more we produce, consume, and recycle plastics, the more plastic will come into the world and accumulate in landfills, on land, in rivers, and the sea. Plastics at sea concentrate incredibly dangerous chemicals, fish eat plastic, and we eat fish.

It's really that simple. This is why we care. It sure as hell isn't for the paycheck.

Texas-Sized Garbage Patches

The garbage patch in the North Pacific isn't the size of Texas, but what [Marc] Gunther suggests in his piece ["In Defense of Plastic Bags," GreenBiz, December 28, 2011,] about the activist role in perpetuating that myth isn't accurate either. Though [Oregon State University oceanography professor quoted by Gunther] Angelique White's assessment is right, she's not quoting her own data to debunk the myth she's talking about (let alone the data from the cruise she was on). What's interesting is that environmentalists were blamed for perpetuating the Lonestar State garbage island myth. White issued a press release through Oregon State University meant to debunk the Texas myth. We the environmentalists, applaud this effort. We can't win with money, so we better have bulletproof facts on our side. What I take issue with is Gunther's snarky tone, where he names the Surfrider Foundation and Heal the Bay as environmental groups spreading misinformation. In Gunther's piece, he copies the line from the press release verbatim: "participated in one of the few expeditions solely aimed at understanding the abundance of plastic debris."

What's interesting is the title of the press release: "Garbage Patch Not Nearly as Big as Media Portrayed." What's ironic is that the press release is unequivocally calling his profession out, not mine. So, in the spirit of Gunther's eye-for-an-eye tactic, is it fair for me to say that the media is responsible for spreading misinformation about the efficacy of plastic bag recycling? I'd say that's accurate. . . .

What We Know

But let's talk about what we do know, rather than beat up on each other and rely on bad journalism and skewed interpretations of press releases for our facts. After three expeditions in the last year, the 5 Gyres Institute has confirmed its suspicions that plastic pollution exists in all major gyres; we will soon be publishing data on plastic pollution density in the South Atlantic and South Pacific gyre.

To date, the largest data set that exists regarding plastic pollution in any area of the ocean is published by SEA Education, which documents 22 years of ocean surface sampling in the North Atlantic and Caribbean, including the western part of the North Atlantic Gyre. The largest concentration of plastics ever recorded is 580,000 plastic particles [each weighing 0.15 gram] per square kilometer which is equal to 87 kilograms (or roughly 191 pounds).

Now, SEA's data set, like almost all data sets on the subject, account only for the plastic that floats. If you talk to scientists about the issue casually, they tend to believe that the density of plastic in the ocean is much higher than their data suggests and that much more research is needed to accurately portray how much plastic is in the ocean, if that's even possible. What scientists know is that there are 7 billion people on earth addicted to plastic and no matter where they look, even in the most remote of places, they find a plastic stain. When I spoke with Kara Lavender Law from SEA Education this spring [2011] about her massive data set, which is the envy of many scientists within this community, she stated plainly that it's still a very small snapshot.

So How Much Is Out There?

Everyone wants to know that answer to this question. According the scientific literature, the best guess so far comes from a report by Columbia University that takes all of the major existing data sets, mixes them with a bit of computer modeling and estimates the ocean surface area of all five major gyres. That number is just shy of 16 million square kilometers, which gives us an estimate of 73,878,000 pounds of plastic within the border of the gyres.

But here's another problem. We're only talking about the gyres. There are 315 million square kilometers of ocean surface on planet earth. From firsthand experience on three research expeditions that have sampled inside and outside the elusive borders of the gyres, I can say this, anecdotally: The gyres do concentrate plastic, but plastic is not just within the gyre borders, it's everywhere. Plastic in the ocean varies in density, but not frequency. Ninety-nine out of 100 times you sample, you'll find plastic, even if you're just a few miles out to sea. So what's in the other 300 million square kilometers of ocean that comprises 65% of the earth's surface? Answer: We don't know. Yikes.

Here's another problem: Much of the plastic doesn't float. PVC, PET, and PS all sink, and the science community has almost no idea how much plastic is on the ocean floor because sampling sediment in 15,000 feet of water is incredibly expensive, if even possible.

Are There Plastic Bags in Gyres?

What's the most common type of plastic found on the surface? LDPE, HDPE, and PP. Gunther defends the plastic bag in his piece without understanding how plastic bags behave in the environment when exposed to the elements. He states plainly that the garbage patches aren't composed of plastic bags. According to the Ocean Conservancy's annual report, 11% of beach litter is plastic bags, even if you don't see it in the picture he provides.

But what happens when a plastic bag enters the ocean? As stated before, plastic doesn't biodegrade in any meaningful timeframe, but it photo-degrades. Thin, flimsy plastic like HDPE with a lot of surface area (like the common bag from grocery stores) photo-degrades faster than thicker plastic. Ultraviolet rays from the sun break the polymer chains of hydrocarbon molecules into smaller pieces and what you end up with is small fragments like the .15g pieces 5 Gyres, Scripps, Algalita and SEA finds in their nets.

Susan Freinkel, author of *Plastic: A Toxic Love Story*, explains this concept well in an analogy from her book. Think of plastic as you would a pearl necklace: the hydrocarbon molecules are the pearls, and the string that holds them together are the polymer chains. Comparatively, the pearls are strong and the string is weak. The sun and the sea attack the string in between.

In short, you might not find a Hilex Poly [a leading plastic bag manufacturer] bag in the "garbage patch" but you surely will find the residue of Hilex Poly's business model there. Doesn't it stand to reason that the biggest culprits of marine plastic pollution are going to come from the most ubiquitously consumed plastic products—indeed, ones that tend to blow in the wind?

Paper or Plastic?

In the pantheon of meaningless comparisons, plastic vs. paper has become the main talking point of plastic industry people. First up, why are we comparing a gunshot wound to cancer? Unchecked, they'll both kill you. But here's the real dilemma: Life-cycle analyses of paper vs. plastic are inconclusive and do not take into account the full range of vectors needed to ad-

"We're trying to discourage carrier bag use."

equately compare the two. Fifty-page reports, like the one Gunther cites in his piece, with a lot of pie charts and graphs, may look convincing, but they still don't pass the sniff test upon closer examination. Reports are based on data sets, and if we don't know, let alone comprehend, how bad the plastic pollution situation is in our world's oceans, how can we factor the impact of plastic bags into a report? We can't. All we know is that we use a whole helluva a lot of them, they fly, and 11% of the trash on the beach worldwide is plastic bags.

Depending on which life-cycle analysis one cites, paper often comes out as the larger greenhouse gas emitter—this is important, as CO_2 emissions are making our oceans more acidic and warming the planet. But the study that Gunther cites is from the UK, which means geographically, it can't be applied to a country as large as the USA in terms of attempting to capture emissions from transportation costs or end-of-life emissions and disposal-cost economics.

Beyond the report's geographic difference, it doesn't account for the fact that we have the technology to make a 100% recycled content paper bags from 100% recycled paper bags from a renewable resource, trees—and you don't have to cut down forests to get paper stock!

Here's the important distinction about paper and plastic recyclability: According to Mark Daniels of Hilex Poly, only 30% post-consumer HDPE can be used to make a new bag, which means 70% of a "recycled" plastic bag comes from virgin sources (non-renewable natural gas, he says). If we apply the laws of mathematics to our axiom, we get this: For every plastic bag you recycle, you create 3.3 more, as a result. And sometimes, recycled HDPE gets downcycled into other products like decking materials. The problem is that plastic decking materials have a lifespan too, and no strategy for reclaiming them at the end of that lifespan has been introduced. If the goal is to reduce plastic accumulation in the environment and the ocean, is creating more plastic from existing plastic the best idea?

What about natural gas—that nice blue flame? It is becoming scarcer. According to the US Energy Information Administration, 35% of domestic Natural Gas mining comes from fracking, and will reach 47% by 2035. Though natural gas burns cleaner than other fossil fuels, getting it out of the ground by fracking creates potent greenhouse gas emissions of methane. According to a congressional report released in April, the 14 biggest fracking companies released 3 billion liters of fracking fluid into the environment, including 29 chemicals known or suspected to be carcinogenic to humans. This is where your plastic bag comes from—or at least 70% of it.

What about all the costs to taxpayers, and CO_2 emissions associated with cleanup of bags in sewers that block drainage and cause floods? One analysis I did found that it cost taxpayers 17 cents per plastic bag to remove them from LA watersheds.

The fact that plastics concentrate dangerous chemicals isn't yet figured in. According to a Scripps study, 9% of "garbage patch" fish showed evidence of plastic ingestion—the fish that serve as food-chain fish for the ones we eat are eating little toxic plastic bombs.

What of the untold cost to wildlife? These are not quantifiable, but if you like sea turtles, then you should be bringing your own bag.

Another Sinister Ploy

Perhaps worried that the reusable bag companies might bite into Hilex's bottom line, Daniels and friends decided to sue California-based reusable bag maker, Chicobag, but later dropped the suit after Chicobag CEO Andy Keller called out the veracity of Hilex's recycling claims. . . .

In addition to bullying social entrepreneurs who try to address the problem, Hilex has also tried to scare consumers about the dangers of reusable bags by funding a study (through the American Chemistry Council's Progressive Bag Affiliates, of which Hilex is a member) on bacterial contamination of reusable bags. The study found that 12% of their whopping 84-bag sample size found E. coli, and all but one contained bacteria. This finding spawned scary headlines in newspapers like the *Washington Post* that read Reusable Bags Found To Be Full Of Bacteria.

But here's the problem: None of the bacteria, or the strains of E. coli present in reusable bags are harmful to humans. And Hilex knows this, though that didn't prevent the company from spinning the report to the media to create a Texas-sized panic. Thankfully, the study was officially debunked by Consumer Reports. My favorite gem from the article comes from senior staff scientist at Consumer Reports, who said, "A person eating an average bag of salad greens gets more exposure to these bacteria than if they had licked the insides of the dirtiest bag from this study." That should effectively end the debate.

Why Not Recycle?

Never mind the admission provided by Hilex Poly that demonstrates that they can't make a plastic bag out of a plastic bag. Let's talk about recycling rates and the skewing of the data done to serve Hilex's own interests.

First up, HDPE is worthless unless you live next door to Hilex Poly. Gunther says that Hilex pays $300–$400 per ton for mixed films, bags and wraps. What he doesn't mention is that this price is paid for the stuff when it's bailed and delivered. But in most cases, it costs more to deliver the plastic to recycling facilities than the plastic is worth. Ask your grocery store where the plastic bags go that you redeem for recycling. Follow the chain of custody. Nine times out of 10, it's probably a dead-end, destined for a landfill—or worse. for a slow boat to China, to be burned for fuel. It's not being recycled.

Gunther also says that Hilex wishes it could get more plastic. Said Mark Daniels, "It is less expensive for us to collect, purchase, transport and reprocess that materials (sic) to all of our other plants than it is to purchase virgin materials." Perhaps they should fire their CFO and their VP of Operations. The supply side of this business model outweighs the demand side by a massive amount, which means the economic model is bad. If the economics are so good around the Hilex model, and indeed plastic was as valuable as Daniels states, why is Hilex importing virgin plastic bags from China to sell to their customers, when there are stacks and stacks upon stacks of clean HDPE and LDPE all over the country that he could be buying?

A quick look at import records for the company showed at least three instances of Hilex importing plastic bags, some of which were sold to Kroger grocery stores in Kansas. . . .

Plastic Bag Recycling Is Low

I'm also curious about Daniels' apparently jittery board of directors, who may be worried about investing in recycling when they can't even begin to handle the existing plastic in the US. What probably makes their directors jittery is this: Hilex Poly has no idea how many plastic bags they recycle and if they do, they're not telling. They are making claims, however, which are false. In one of Hilex's blog posts they claim that "PE recycling of bags, wraps and films is up to 15%!" Note that they don't say, "HDPE" recycling rates, which are actually, down. Truth is, bags, films, and wraps are not sorted by Hilex or anyone else. My guess, which is good as anyone's, including Hilex's and the EPA's, is that fewer than 1% of plastic bags are recycled.

Had Gunther read page 9 of the EPA report on which he hinges his entire argument for saving the plastic bag, he'd notice that recycling rates for HDPE aren't going up, they're dropping. In 2010, the recycling rate for HDPE was 4.3%, compared to 6.1% in 2009. Curiously, the 15% total capture rate that Hilex cites isn't even in this report.

That plastics bags are 100% recyclable isn't the issue. It's that by a massive percentage they are not recycled. Even when they are, we end up with more plastic in the environment instead of less. And if we believe we're making modest gains in plastic bag recycling each year—which we're not—consumption rates far outpace recycling rates.

Furthermore, why are we investing in a system that has to fabricate bag recycling rates to trend positively, even though the fabricated trend still amounts for next to nothing? What society accepts a 4.3% efficacy rate in any system without abandoning it and going back to the drawing board? When it comes to plastic bags, there's only one thing to do that's 100% effective: Ban them.

If Mark Daniels wants environmentalists to go hand in hand with him into the meadow, and Marc Gunther wants to feel good about his hybrid full of plastic bags, they might want to quit insulting our intelligence. Environmentalists will come to the table, because we understand how damaging to this Earth plastic bags are.

But until you become a transparent, objective force for change, the bag bans will keep coming at breakneck speed. We might not have the money on our side, but we have something that always wins in the end: the truth.

> *"Banning the bags may actually be a net negative for the environment, yielding little benefit to wildlife while significantly increasing carbon emissions and other environmental impacts."*

Plastic Bag Bans Do Not Protect the Environment

Todd Myers

Todd Myers is an author and the environmental director of the Washington Policy Center. In the following viewpoint, he says that banning plastic bags would not help the environment and would in fact harm it. Advocates of a ban, he asserts, are relying upon inappropriate data and circulating misleading or false information. Even leading environmental advocacy groups like Greenpeace, he points out, do not feel that banning plastic bags is the best approach to dealing with plastic waste. When the energy used to create and use plastic bags was compared to the energy used to create and use paper or reusable cotton bags, plastic bags were found to require the lowest amount of energy; given this, he says, banning plastic bags in favor of paper or reusable bags would actually increase energy use. Instead of choosing to ban plastic bags, he concludes, communities should pay attention to the science and choose policies that would lead to actual re-ductions in negative environmental impact.

As you read, consider the following questions:

1. According to the author, how many marine mammals were a city council in Washington state told were killed by either plastic ingestion or entanglement?

2. What did oceanography professor Angel White say in a press release in 2011, according to Myers?

3. How many times would a consumer have to use a reus-able cotton bag before breaking even with plastic bags from an energy-use standpoint, according to Myers?

A cross the country, cities are joining the latest environ-mental trend—banning plastic grocery bags. Concerned about the amount of plastic that reaches our oceans and the impact on wildlife, communities have decided that banning the bags is a simple and environmentally responsible approach.

But is it? What does the science say?

The evidence points to the fact that banning the bags may actually be a net negative for the environment, yielding little benefit to wildlife while significantly increasing carbon emis-sions and other environmental impacts.

Advocates of banning plastic grocery bags often cite im-pacts on marine life and mammals, but they rarely attempt to quantify that impact. Unfortunately, many attempts to quan-tify those impacts are simply false or misleading. For example, one city council in Washington state was told "the ecological impacts of this plastic include over a million seabirds and 100,000 marine mammals killed by either plastic ingestions or entanglement."

Plastic Bags Are Not to Blame

In fact, the claim about harm to marine mammals and seabirds has nothing to do with plastic bags. NOAA [National Oceanic and Atmospheric Administration] corrected the claim about seabirds on its web page saying, "We are so far unable to find a scientific reference for this figure." The only study NOAA can find does not deal with plastic bags or even marine debris, but "*active* fishing gear bycatch," in other words, fishing nets that are being used at sea, not discarded plastic bags.

The Times of London addressed this very issue in 2008, even quoting a Greenpeace biologist saying, "It's very unlikely that many animals are killed by plastic bags. The evidence shows just the opposite. We are not going to solve the problem of waste by focusing on plastic bags."

One of the most commonly heard claims is that plastic bags, and other plastic, have created the "Pacific Garbage Patch." Some claim it is twice the size of Texas. This is simply false. Last year [2011], Oregon State University reported that the actual amount is less than one percent the size of Texas. Oceanography professor Angel White sent out a release last year saying, "There is no doubt that the amount of plastic in the world's oceans is troubling, but this kind of exaggeration undermines the credibility of scientists."

Additionally, White notes that the amount of plastic in the ocean hasn't been increasing. For example, the Wood's Hole Oceanographic Institute found the amount of plastic in the Atlantic Ocean hasn't increased since the 1980s.

This doesn't mean plastic bags cause no impact. When determining the environmental costs and benefits, however, we need to be honest about the science.

Bans Pose Environmental Risks

Indeed, there are risks from banning plastic grocery bags.

The most significant environmental risk from banning plastic bags is the increase in energy use. Plastic bags are the most energy-efficient form of grocery bag. The U.K. Environment Agency compared energy use for plastic, paper and reusable bags. It found the "global warming potential" of plastic grocery bags is one-fourth that of paper bags and 1/173rd that of a reusable cotton bag. In other words, consumers would have to use a reusable cotton bag 173 times before they broke even from an energy standpoint. Thus, even if consumers switched to reusable bags, it is not clear there would be a reduced environmental impact.

Ironically, many of the cities leading the charge against plastic bags are signatories to the U.S. Conference of Mayors Climate Protection Agreement. Yet, few of these cities even attempt to assess the climate impact of switching from the least energy-intensive grocery bag to bags that use far more energy to produce.

The U.K. Environment Agency study is echoed by other research as well, and the reason is simple—grocery stores began using plastic bags in part because they are cheaper to produce, in part because they use less energy to manufacture.

Finally, it should be noted that the benefit of banning plastic bags is mitigated by the fact that half of the bags are used for other purposes, like for garbage bags or for picking up after pets. Grocery shoppers will still have to buy other bags, likely plastic, for those purposes.

In the end, communities need to sincerely weigh these various environmental costs. Unfortunately, few do any analysis because the political symbolism of banning the bags is powerful. It is often easier to ignore the science that indicates such bans may actually harm the environment than make an honest effort to weigh these difficult issues.

This is why plastic bag bans have become more environmental fad than environmental benefit.

> "*[Extended producer responsibility] systems can lead to profits in processing used materials, reductions in carbon emissions and energy used to produce packaging, and thousands of new 'green' jobs.*"

Extended Producer Responsibility Mandates Benefit the Environment and Businesses

Conrad MacKerron

Conrad MacKerron is senior director at the environmental nonprofit group As You Sow and an experienced shareholder advocacy engagement leader for social and environmental policies at publicly traded companies. In the following viewpoint, MacKerron argues that mandating extended producer responsibility (EPR)—policies that shift financial responsibility for collecting and recycling used packaging—would help to reduce waste, increase recycling, and help US businesses realize profits in reclaimed materials. MacKerron outlines several key economic and environmental benefits of EPR laws, and asserts that businesses

*that produce packaging should assume responsibility for collect-
ing and recycling it; the recycling goals and timelines for implementation should be aggressive; and a national EPR program
should be mandated by the US government and financed and
managed by businesses.*

As you read, consider the following questions:

1. How many jetliners does Alcoa say could be built with
   material wasted annually in the United States, according
   to the author?

2. How many US cities does MacKerron say have banned
   or restricted the use of polystyrene food packaging?

3. What year did the European Union enact a packaging
   waste directive, according to MacKerron?

Americans generate more waste than any other country in
the world but recycle far less than other developed coun-
ties like Denmark, Belgium, or Germany. Post-consumer paper and paperboard and packaging, which together form the
largest category of municipal solid waste, merit priority attention in efforts to improve extremely poor recycling rates for
many post-consumer materials. Shifting financial responsibility for collecting and recycling used packaging in the U.S.
from taxpayers to producers through a policy known as "extended producer responsibility" (EPR) will incentivize producers to reduce the amount of packaging they create, substantially increase recycling rates, provide much needed revenue to
improve efficiency of recycling systems, reduce carbon footprint and energy use, and reclaim billions of dollars of embedded value now buried in landfills.

Post-consumer paper and paperboard and packaging consist of valuable commodities such as aluminum, glass, paper,
plastic, and steel. A new estimate completed by As You Sow
concludes that the market value of these materials that are not

recycled in the U.S. was $11.4 billion in 2010. It is not good business practice to throw away valuable resources.

We live in a world of finite, dwindling resources. Businesses that do not develop sustainable sourcing of products through resource-efficient circular, or closed loop, systems in the very near term, will not be able to compete to serve a world population estimated at nine billion by 2050.

Recycling Rates for Packaging Lag

U.S. packaging recycling rates lag behind other developed countries by significant amounts. Denmark has an 84% packaging recycling rate, Belgium is at 78%, the Netherlands at 72%, Germany at 73%. The U.S. recovery rate is estimated at 48.3% for packaging and 52.7% for paper and paperboard products. There are some bright spots; the U.S. does well in paper recycling, but aside from paper, just 22% of remaining packaging is recycled. Only 12.1% of plastic packaging, the dominant packaging of the future, is recycled, There are other troubling trends: beverage container recycling rates have dropped 20% over the last two decades. One quarter of the U.S. population still doesn't have access to curbside recycling. More than 40 billion aluminum cans, the most valuable beverage container material, are still dumped annually into landfills in the U.S. According to Alcoa, this wasted material could provide enough aluminum to build 25,000 jetliners!

Our locally controlled and taxpayer-funded recycling collection systems are often ill-equipped to deal with increasing volume and an expanding array of packaging wastes. Saddled with projected deficits topping $100 billion, local governments cannot afford to invest in improving recycling systems. Over 47 countries require producers to bear some or all of the cost of end-of-life packaging management that in the U.S. has always been paid for by taxpayers. As You Sow believes it is time to shift financial responsibility for managing packaging to producers through effective and tested EPR policies.

EPR laws and policies are already firmly established in the U.S. for several product categories. More than 70 producer responsibility laws are in effect in 32 states, covering batteries, mobile phones, paint, pesticide containers, carpet, electronics, thermostats, and fluorescent lamps—but not packaging. Twenty-three states have passed EPR laws requiring technology makers to take responsibility for end-of-life management of electronics.

Container deposit laws, structured as EPR programs in eight of the 10 states that have them, are a major success story. The U.S. recycling rate for beverage containers is only 35%, but in the 10 states with deposit laws, recycling rates range from 66% to 96%. However, these laws have not expanded to apply to other kinds of consumer packaging.

Incentives to Save

Shifting financial responsibility to producers for packaging can lead to internalization of end-of-life costs, resulting in economic incentives to reduce packaging and a transition to easier to recycle materials. Efficiently designed and administered EPR systems can lead to profits in processing used materials, reductions in carbon emissions and energy used to produce packaging, and thousands of new "green" jobs in collection and processing.

There is also a need for greater focus on plastics, which have come to dominate the packaging sector and pose special challenges. There is a growing link between ineffective waste management and plastic debris, which is piling up in the Earth's ocean gyres where it injures and kills marine life, can transport invasive species, and potentially poses a threat to human health. A recent assessment of marine debris concluded that a substantial cause of this debris entering the sea is inadequate waste management infrastructure and inappropriate disposal. Concern about ocean plastic has resulted in more than 60 cities in California and 100 cities in the U.S.

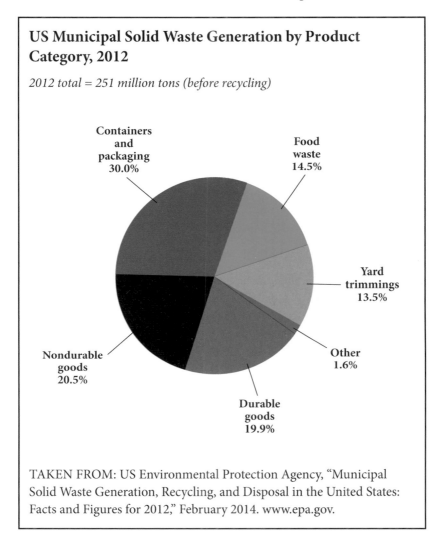

US Municipal Solid Waste Generation by Product Category, 2012

2012 total = 251 million tons (before recycling)

Containers and packaging 30.0%

Food waste 14.5%

Yard trimmings 13.5%

Other 1.6%

Durable goods 19.9%

Nondurable goods 20.5%

TAKEN FROM: US Environmental Protection Agency, "Municipal Solid Waste Generation, Recycling, and Disposal in the United States: Facts and Figures for 2012," February 2014. www.epa.gov.

banning or restricting use of polystyrene foam food packaging and another 28 California municipalities banning plastic take-out bags.

Extended Producer Responsibility Laws

EPR laws would resolve many of the concerns identified with packaging recycling by:

- Substantially increasing recovery rates for all post-consumer packaging

- Incentivizing producers to redesign packaging to reduce materials and improve recyclability

- Creating the potential for profitable secondary materials markets for the more than $11 billion worth of packaging that was landfilled in 2010 alone

- Providing stable revenue sources through producer fees to improve the curbside recycling infrastructure and build new systems to collect waste from consumers when away from home

- Reducing greenhouse gases

  Nestlé Waters North America says 55% of its carbon footprint comes from production of its bottles and that recycling a bottle reduces its greenhouse gas impact by 25%

- Meeting pent up demand for recyclables

  There is enormous demand for recycled PET plastic used for soda and water bottles, yet recyclers have been unable to increase supplies with existing recycling programs; PET recycling rates languish at a paltry 29%

  U.S. recycled PET makers urgently need more materials so major brands can meet commitments made to use high levels of recycled package content

The European Union [EU] enacted a packaging waste directive in 1994, requiring member states to develop systems to meet recycling goals. Most chose EPR-based systems. Europen, a packaging industry trade group, calls the directive "clearly one of the most successful pieces of EU environmental legislation," responsible for a "remarkable" reduction in waste sent to disposal and for "lower costs for the public purse." The amount of packaging going to final disposal in 15 EU countries fell by 43% over the past 11 years, largely due to higher recycling levels.

In the last two years, momentum has been building for introduction of EPR for packaging in the U.S. This has been driven by the factors cited above. Working with a group of aligned shareholders, As You Sow has led engagement of major consumer goods and grocery companies to adopt EPR polices. These companies include Colgate-Palmolive, General Mills, Kraft Foods, Safeway, Supervalu, Target, Kroger, Procter & Gamble, Unilever, Walmart, Ahold USA, and Whole Foods. Surprisingly, prominent companies are among those calling for producers to take responsibility for packaging—most notably Coca-Cola and Nestlé Waters. For the emerging EPR effort to build sufficient traction, other large companies must step up and take responsibility. A new non-governmental organization, Recycling Reinvented, is serving as a policy strategy center for educating stakeholders and to move EPR for packaging legislation in U.S. states. Among its board members is renowned environmental leader Robert F. Kennedy Jr.

- Businesses that place substantial amounts of packaging on the U.S. market should take responsibility for collecting and recycling post-consumer packaging.

- Companies should prioritize engagement with peers and other stakeholders to reach agreement on binding state producer responsibility legislation setting high packaging recycling goals for all individual kinds of packaging (75%+) and an aggressive timeline for meeting them.

- A successful mandated EPR for packaging program in the U.S. should address all packaging types, be financed and managed by producers, drive source reduction, require participation by all businesses that produce packaging waste, and phase out use of non-recyclable packaging.

- By supporting EPR laws and policies that drive more aggressive and effective collection efforts, companies can then make commitments to use far higher levels of recycled content in product packaging, which, in turn, supports a circular system ensuring a stable supply of post-consumer materials to use as new feedstock.

State-of-the-art mining of our post-consumer packaging "trash" is a crucial step to propel us towards sustainable production and consumption policies that will ease the stress on our planet's limited natural resources and help feed, clothe, and shelter a world population of nine billion people by 2050.

| "Companies' biggest gripe about [extended producer responsibility] laws is not their cost but their inconsistency."

Extended Producer Responsibility Spreads: Junk Bond

The Economist

The Economist *is a weekly newspaper that focuses on international politics and business news. The following viewpoint discusses the difficulties companies are experiencing with extended producer responsibility (EPR) laws. Some concerns, the author points out, deal with the inherent costs to the companies for waste disposal. The issue then becomes, according to the viewpoint, that the costs would ultimately be passed on to the consumer—but not all companies share this view. In fact, the author states, certain companies in states without EPR laws have preemptively set up a waste disposal program, hoping to get ahead of impending legislation. The author concludes that the biggest concern companies have with EPR is the inconsistency of how the law is applied in each state.*

As you read, consider the following questions:

1. How many US states have product-specific EPR laws, according to the viewpoint?

2. What does the author say that the California Chamber of Commerce calls EPR bills? Why?

3. How are some companies in states without EPR bills reacting, according to the viewpoint?

For seasoned shoppers, "buyer's remorse" is a familiar feeling. "Seller's remorse" may also become common soon, as ever more governments order manufacturers to assume the cost of disposing of their products after consumers are done with them. Until recently, most laws on "extended producer responsibility" (EPR) or "product stewardship" applied only to specific types of goods, such as car tyres or electronics. But in late March Maine, following the lead of several Canadian provinces, became the first American state to enact a blanket EPR law, which could in principle cover any product.

Governments are eager to unload some responsibility for waste management onto manufacturers, especially for products that are hard to recycle or may be toxic, such as electronics, batteries, paint, car parts and pesticide containers. It helps them cut costs, for one thing—handy for local authorities short of cash in the recession. In Maine, which has had an EPR law for electronic waste since 2004, municipalities save $1.5m–3m annually because manufacturers have picked up the cost of collection, according to the Natural Resources Council of Maine. Governments also hope that EPR laws will encourage firms to rethink the way they make products, designing them for longevity and recyclability rather than for the landfill.

Thirty-one of America's 50 states have product-specific EPR laws. The European Union requires manufacturers to dispose of packaging, electronics and vehicles. Canada and Japan also have EPR laws. Other countries, such as Australia, have flirted with the idea.

Maine's new "framework" law makes it much easier to expand the scope of EPR schemes, by establishing a process for adding products to the list of those covered without requiring a new law each time. The state government, which already enforces five product-specific EPR laws, is now said to have carpet-makers and drugs firms in its sights.

This worries businesses, few of which are eager to pick up the bill for waste disposal. Some business associations, such as the California Chamber of Commerce, have denounced EPR bills as "job killers". They point out that the increased costs are ultimately borne by consumers. But that does not worry supporters of EPR, who argue that the price of a product should reflect its full "life-cycle" costs, including disposal, rather than simply leaving taxpayers to make up the difference. Moreover, unless manufacturers are forced to bear the costs, they will have no incentive to make their wares easy to dispose of.

Scott Cassel, executive director of the Product Stewardship Institute, a non-profit organisation, says he has noticed different "stages of grief for companies" coping with the reality of EPR, starting with denial and moving to begrudging acceptance. Not all companies are mourning, however. Some manufacturers and retailers have voluntarily rolled out collection programmes in states that do not require them. Hewlett-Packard, a technology firm, claims to design its products with ease of recycling in mind—cradle-to-cradle, as the jargon has it. Staples, which sells office supplies, and Home Depot, a home-improvement retailer, both offer national take-back programmes in their stores for such items as computer monitors, compact fluorescent light bulbs and batteries. Such programmes may enhance customer loyalty, particularly among environmentally conscious consumers.

Some companies may also be hoping that starting their own collection programmes could help them pre-empt legislation. "We thought we could get out in front of this and set up a system to collect our products, and the exact opposite happened," says Doug Smith of Sony, an electronics giant. He does not believe EPR laws have much impact on product design.

Companies' biggest gripe about EPR laws is not their cost but their inconsistency. Few states have the same requirements, making compliance complicated for manufacturers. Many businesses would favour a national policy rather than a patchwork of local laws. EPR laws, it seems, are set to win extended responsibility themselves.

Periodical and Internet Sources Bibliography

The following articles have been selected to supplement the diverse views presented in this chapter.

Allison Chan	"Banning Plastic Bags: It Works," EcoSalon, March 2, 2013. http://ecosalon.com.
Jaimee Lynn Fletcher and Joanna Clay	"Advocates Press for Clear Look at Plastic-Bag Bans," *Orange County Register*, February 15, 2013.
Andrew Hutson	"CEOs Want Pro-sustainability Policies? They Need to Speak Up," Environmental Defense Fund, November 26, 2013. www.edf.org.
Robb Krehbiel and Emma Jornlin	"Cutting Down on Plastic: Bag Bans Prove Popular and Successful," Environment Washington, December 2012. www.environmentwashington.org.
Chris Plecash	"'Green Economy' Rhetoric Muddying Policy Waters, Say Economists," *Hill Times* Online, December 2, 2013. www.hilltimes.com.
Ian A. Thaure	"Globalism and Electronic Waste: Why Electronic Waste Trade Is Bad for Both Parties," Bard Center for Civic Engagement, August 6, 2013. http://blogs.bard.edu.
Michael Washburn	"Executive Perspective: U.S. Recycling Not Meeting Industry Demand: Here's How to Fix It," Sustainability, June 18, 2013. http://sustainability.thomsonreuters.com.
Timothy Whitehouse	"E-waste Exports: Why the National Strategy for Electronics Stewardship Does Not Go Far Enough," *Journal of Energy & Environmental Law*, Winter 2012.

For Further Discussion

Chapter 1

1. Brian Parham contends that we are facing numerous environmental challenges that amount to a global environmental crisis but that even though the evidence seems grim and overwhelming, it is important to remain hopeful that the problems will be addressed before catastrophic events take place. Michael Barone contends that those who believe that global warming constitutes an environmental "crisis," particularly in light of the fact that the planet has not warmed in the last fifteen years or to the extent predicted, are essentially the same as religious zealots who deny reality in the service of their faith. Which author do you think presents the more accurate representation of scientific facts, and why? Cite from the viewpoints in your answer.

Chapter 2

1. Arthur R. Williams argues that the only reason that nuclear energy is not more widely viewed as a safe and suitable form of renewable energy that can help reduce carbon emissions is that erroneous "myths" about nuclear energy have become accepted as reality. Friends of the Earth maintains that nuclear energy presents too many safety threats and that other forms of renewable energy used in combination can supply the same amount of energy as nuclear more economically and without the risks. What do you think about nuclear energy? Do the viewpoints address the questions that you have about the safety, reliability, and sustainability of green energy? If not, then what kind of information do you think you would need in order to make a truly informed decision about supporting nuclear energy?

2. Does the viewpoint by the Nongovernmental International Panel on Climate Change influence your opinion of Barack Obama's contention that carbon emissions should be reduced? Why or why not? Provide examples from both viewpoints to support your answer.

Chapter 3

1. Bill Freeman contends that special interest groups with a vested interest in other forms of alternative energy are deliberately spreading misinformation about the hazards of fracking. Food and Water Watch contends that groups that represent the interests of the companies that profit from fracking are deliberately covering up the dangers inherent in the process. Does referring to the motivations of the groups that oppose them help to bolster the viewpoint authors' credibility or make you suspicious of their own motivations? Given what you have read, do you think that fracking is a safe and sustainable practice? Explain your reasoning.

2. Rod Smith refutes the claims made by the United Nations Global Environmental Alert Service (UNGEAS) that modern animal agriculture is a major contributor to greenhouse gas emissions. Does Smith provide adequate facts and figures to support his claim? Does the UNGEAS? After reading both viewpoints, can you confidently determine the extent to which animal agriculture's greenhouse gas emissions are contributing to climate change? Cite from the viewpoints that you used to arrive at your conclusion.

Chapter 4

1. Does Todd Myers's statement about the amount of energy needed to produce paper or cotton bags vs. plastic bags seem persuasive in light of what Stiv Wilson says about the science used to compare the impact of plastic bags vs.

paper bags? Which author provides better support for his argument? Explain your answer. Do you think that plastic bags should be banned? Why or why not?

2. After reading the viewpoints by Conrad MacKerron and *The Economist*, do you think that mandating extended producer responsibility policies will benefit the environment? Why or why not?

Organizations to Contact

The editors have compiled the following list of organizations concerned with the issues debated in this book. The descriptions are derived from materials provided by the organizations. All have publications or information available for interested readers. The list was compiled on the date of publication of the present volume; names, addresses, phone and fax numbers, and e-mail and Internet addresses may change. Be aware that many organizations take several weeks or longer to respond to inquiries, so allow as much time as possible.

Americans Against Fracking
(202) 683-4905
e-mail: kfried@fwwatch.org
website: www.americansagainstfracking.org

Americans Against Fracking is a coalition of local, state, and national civic groups, businesses, faith-based institutions, hospitals and other health institutions, professional associations, labor unions, political clubs, environmental organizations, social justice groups, farms, restaurants, breweries, and other food producers that support a national ban on drilling and fracking for oil and natural gas in order to protect natural resources. The group supports federal, state, and local efforts to ban fracking and to enact moratoriums and to stop practices that facilitate fracking. The group's website contains links to its various members' websites as well as information on fracking provided by Food and Water Watch.

America's Natural Gas Alliance (ANGA)
701 Eighth Street NW, Suite 800, Washington, DC   20001
(202) 789-2642
e-mail: info@anga.us
website: www.anga.us

America's Natural Gas Alliance represents independent natural gas exploration and production companies. ANGA aims to increase awareness of the economic, environmental, and national security benefits of natural gas. ANGA promotes the benefits of natural gas to a wide range of audiences, including electric power utilities, nongovernmental organizations, and federal and state policy makers and regulators.

Earth Justice

426 Seventeenth Street, 6th Floor, Oakland, CA   94612
(800) 584-6460 • fax: (510) 550-6740
e-mail: info@earthjustice.org
website: earthjustice.org

Earth Justice is a nonprofit public interest law firm that fights for environmental justice and the full implementation of environmental laws and regulations. The organization has provided legal representation to a number of conservation and environmental groups, including the Natural Resources Defense Council (NRDC), the Sierra Club, and the Wilderness Society. It also lobbies to strengthen federal environmental laws and create policies that will protect endangered species and undeveloped lands. Earth Justice publishes a monthly e-newsletter, *e.Brief*, that explores relevant environmental issues and provides updates on recent cases. The Earth Justice website offers access to the latest press releases and *Unearthed*, a blog that shares the latest news and facilitates discussion on environmental and legal topics.

Environmental Defense Fund (EDF)

1875 Connecticut Ave. NW, Suite 600, Washington, DC   20009
(800) 684-3322
e-mail: members@environmentaldefense.org
website: www.edf.org

Established in 1967, the Environmental Defense Fund is a US-based nonprofit environmental advocacy group that focuses on global warming, ecosystem restoration, clean oceans, and human health. Because it was founded by scientists, the EDF is committed to sound scientific research to address environmental problems. One of the areas to which EDF has made a valuable contribution in influencing public policy is the recognition of global climate change as an urgent problem. The EDF website features blogs, podcasts, and commentary on the latest environmental issues, as well as archives of *Solutions*, the EDF's quarterly newsletter.

Greenpeace International

Ottho Heldringstraat 5, Amsterdam, Netherlands   1066 AZ
fax: +31 (0)20 718 2002
e-mail: supporter.services.int@greenpeace.org
website: www.greenpeace.org

Greenpeace is an independent global campaigning organization that acts to change attitudes and behavior in order to protect and conserve the environment and to promote peace. Using sometimes controversial direct-action techniques and a website publishing fact sheets on environmental concerns, Greenpeace strives to educate the public on current environmental issues and policies. Greenpeace publishes fact sheets and reports, as well as a blog on issues pertaining to environmental issues and policies.

International Energy Agency (IEA)

9 rue de la Fédération, Paris, France   75015
+33 1 40 57 6500 • fax: +33 1 40 57 6559
e-mail: info@iea.org
website: www.iea.org

The International Energy Agency is an intergovernmental association that advises its twenty-eight member countries on issues of energy policy and clean energy. The IEA focuses on finding solutions for its members on energy security, economic development, and environmental protection—especially on climate change. It conducts energy research and statistical compilation to assess the current state of the energy market and project future trends in the industry, to disseminate the latest energy news and policy analyses, and to provide well-researched recommendations to member states. The IEA publishes numerous in-depth reports offering insight on the energy industry and specific energy topics, as well as a monthly newsletter, *IEA Open Energy Technology Bulletin*, which provides regular updates on energy security and environmental issues.

Keep America Beautiful (KAB)

1010 Washington Blvd., Stamford, CT 06901
(203) 659-3000 • fax: (203) 659-3001
e-mail: info@kab.org
website: www.kab.org

Keep America Beautiful is a volunteer-based community action and education organization that aims to improve the environment. KAB has developed and implemented programs that bring communities together to generate improved environmental policies and stewardship in three main areas: litter prevention, recycling and waste reduction, and beautification and community greening. Another key activity of KAB is public education programs to raise awareness of recycling and waste reduction. KAB publishes an e-newsletter, *Community Matters*, and the organization's Curbside Value Partnership Program offers a quarterly newsletter, *Bin Buzz*, that can be accessed through the KAB website.

National Oceanic and Atmospheric Administration (NOAA)

1401 Constitution Ave. NW, Room 5128
Washington, DC 20230
(301) 713-1208
e-mail: outreach@noaa.gov
website: www.noaa.gov

The National Oceanic and Atmospheric Administration is a government agency comprising several organizations such as the National Marine Fisheries Service, the National Ocean Service, and the National Weather Service. The agency's goal is to educate the public about environmental issues and to provide services such as daily weather forecasts, severe storm warnings, and climate monitoring to fisheries management, coastal restoration groups, and marine commerce. Almost all agency programs are science and research based and strive to protect life and property and to conserve and protect natural resources.

Natural Resources Defense Council (NRDC)
40 W. Twentieth Street, New York, NY   10011
(212) 727-2700 • fax: (212) 727-1773
website: www.nrdc.org

Established in 1970, the Natural Resources Defense Council is an environmental action organization that mobilizes lawyers, activists, policy makers, and scientists to protect wildlife and the natural environment. The NRDC's aims include reducing waste, improving and facilitating the spread of recycling programs, eliminating the dumping of toxic chemicals and solid waste on land and in the water, and reducing pollution of all kinds. NRDC.tv, which can be accessed on the organization's website, offers video and audio on a range of environmental subjects. The website also hosts *Switchboard*, a blog from NRDC's environmental experts, and *OnEarth*, a blog that covers the latest news from *OnEarth* magazine, a publication that explores major environmental issues and NRDC initiatives.

The Nature Conservancy
4245 N. Fairfax Drive, Suite 100, Arlington, VA   22203-1606
(703) 841-5300
website: www.nature.org

The Nature Conservancy is an environmental organization composed of scientists in the United States and thirty-three other countries. The organization partners with governments around the world, as well as with nonprofit organizations and corporations, to conserve the environment. Its collaborative approach is aimed at finding practical solutions so that nature can continue to provide shelter and sustenance upon which animal and human life depends. The organization encourages individual membership and publishes a regular blog as well as papers and articles on its website.

Nuclear Energy Institute (NEI)

1776 Eye Street NW, Suite 400, Washington, DC   20006
(202) 739-8000 • fax: (202) 785-4019
website: www.nei.org

The Nuclear Energy Institute is a policy organization that works to implement pro-nuclear policies and advocates for the use of nuclear energy and technologies. The NEI is active in developing regulations that benefit both the nuclear industry and communities and in lobbying for pro-nuclear-industry legislation. The organization also raises awareness of the benefits of nuclear power to the public, providing public relations and educational services to promote the industry. The NEI website offers access to a library of documents, including statistics, fact sheets, research papers, policy briefs, and in-depth reports on nuclear power and the nuclear power industry. It also provides a link to the NEI's bimonthly newsletter, *Nuclear Energy Insight*, that examines emerging technologies and policy opinions and updates.

Plastic Pollution Coalition

2150 Allston Way, Suite 460, Berkeley, CA   94704
(510) 394-5772
e-mail: contact@plasticpollutioncoalition.org
website: http://plasticpollutioncoalition.org

The Plastic Pollution Coalition is a network of organizations, businesses, and activists working together to reduce and eventually eliminate pollution caused by disposable plastics. One of its main objectives is to raise awareness of the environmental dangers of plastic pollution and to facilitate a shift to more environmentally responsible practices. Banning plastic bags is a key initiative sponsored by the network. The Plastic Pollution Coalition website links to video of recent lectures, presentations, and speeches on plastic pollution and posts information on upcoming events.

Practice Greenhealth

12335 Sunrise Valley Drive, Suite 680, Reston, VA   20191
(888) 688-3332 • fax: (866) 379-8705
e-mail: info@practicegreenhealth.org
website: www.practicegreenhealth.org

Practice Greenhealth is a membership and networking organization for the health care community. Its primary focus is on developing and encouraging sustainable, environmentally friendly practices for the industry, including the reprocessing of medical equipment. Practice Greenhealth hosts seminars and lectures to disseminate information about the latest eco-friendly strategies in health care, as well as forums to share ideas and collaborate on green initiatives. One such program is Greening the OR, which focuses on products and practices in the operating room that can reduce the amount of waste generated. Practice Greenhealth publishes a weekly e-newsletter, *Greenhealth eNews*, that offers the latest news in the field and updates on ongoing initiatives.

Save the Plastic Bag Coalition

350 Bay Street, Suite 100-328, San Francisco, CA   94133
website: www.savethepasticbag.com

The Save the Plastic Bag Coalition was founded in 2008 to advocate for the use of plastic bags, paper bags, and reusable bags. It presents research on the effect of plastic and paper bag pollution to counter what it sees as anti-plastic-bag propaganda. These studies can be found on the organization's website. Save the Plastic Bag Coalition acts legislatively in its home state of California to ensure that municipalities considering a plastic tax or bag ban does due diligence and that policy makers know the truth about their options. The group's website provides counterpoints to environmental groups that seek to eliminate the use of plastic and paper bags and works to correct misinformation and myths.

Sierra Club

85 Second Street, 2nd Floor, San Francisco, CA   94105
(415) 977-5500 • fax: (415) 977-5799
e-mail: information@sierraclub.org
website: www.sierraclub.org

The Sierra Club is the oldest environmental organization in the United States. Its mission is to protect communities from environmental dangers, including waste pollution. To that end, the Sierra Club has formulated a Climate Recovery Agenda, which it describes as a set of initiatives that will help cut carbon emissions by 80 percent by 2050, reduce US dependence on foreign oil, create a clean-energy economy, and protect the natural heritage, communities, and country from the consequences of global warming. The Sierra Club publishes a range of e-newsletters, including *The Insider*, which is considered the organization's flagship publication. The Sierra Club website links to blogs, videos, the Sierra Club radio station, and other publications, such as *Sierra Magazine*.

Solving the E-waste Problem (StEP)

StEP Secretariat c/o United Nations University
  (UNU-ISP SCYCLE), Bonn   53113
  Germany
+49 (0)228 815-0213 • fax: +49 (0)228 815-0299
e-mail: info@step-initiative.org
website: www.step-initiative.org

Solving the E-waste Problem is an initiative supported by representatives from industry, international organizations, governments, nongovernmental organizations, and academia to address the problem of e-waste. StEP uses scientific assessments and advocates a perspective that takes into account the social, environmental, and economic aspects of e-waste. StEP provides research on electrical and electronic equipment life cycles, as well as their global supply chains and manufacturing processes. StEP opposes illegal activities related to e-waste that present environmental and human-health hazards, and seeks to foster socially responsible, safe, eco-friendly, and energy-efficient recycling and the reuse of electronic equipment and its components worldwide.

United States Environmental Protection Agency (EPA)
Ariel Rios Building, Washington, DC   20004
(202) 272-0167
website: www.epa.gov

The Environmental Protection Agency is a US governmental agency that is tasked with protecting America's natural environment and safeguarding human health. The key responsibility of the EPA is to write and enforce environmental regulations. Established in 1970, the agency also conducts environmental research, provides assessments on environmental problems, and offers education on environmental policy and practices. The EPA works closely with local, state, and tribal governments to offer feedback and guidance on environmental policies and problems. On the EPA website, you can find its monthly newsletter, *Go Green!*; a listing of environmental laws and regulations; updates on recent programs and initiatives; transcripts of speeches, seminars, and congressional testimony; and in-depth research on environmental issues.

Bibliography of Books

Michael L. Bender   *Paleoclimate*. Princeton, NJ: Princeton University Press, 2013.

John J. Berger   *Climate Myths: The Campaign Against Climate Science*. Berkeley, CA: Northbrae Books, 2013.

Eleanor Boyle   *High Steaks: Why and How to Eat Less Meat*. Gabriola Island, BC: New Society, 2012.

Robert Bryce   *Power Hungry: The Myths of "Green" Energy and the Real Fuels of the Future*. New York: PublicAffairs, 2010.

Philip Cafaro and Eileen Crist   *Life on the Brink: Environmentalists Confront Overpopulation*. Athens: University of Georgia Press, 2012.

Canadian Association of Energy and Pipeline Landowner Associations (CAEPLA)   *A Revolution Underground: The History, Economics and Environmental Impacts of Hydraulic Fracturing*. Calgary, AB: CAEPLA, 2012.

Danny Chivers   *The No-Nonsense Guide to Climate Change: The Science, the Solutions, the Way Forward*. 2nd ed. Oxford, UK: New Internationalist, 2011.

Matthew Connelly   *Fatal Misconception: The Struggle to Control World Population*. Cambridge, MA: Belknap, 2008.

Erika Creighton and Paul Danovich, eds.	*Environmental Policy: Management, Legal Issues, and Health Aspects.* Hauppauge, NY: Nova Science, 2013.
James Delingpole	*The Little Green Book of Eco-fascism: The Left's Plan to Frighten Your Kids, Drive Up Energy Costs, and Hike Your Taxes!* Washington, DC: Regnery, 2013.
David Elliott, ed.	*Nuclear or Not? Does Nuclear Power Have a Place in a Sustainable Energy Future?* New York: Palgrave Macmillan, 2007.
Stephen Emmott	*Ten Billion.* New York: Vintage, 2013.
Daniel C. Esty and Andrew S. Winston	*Green to Gold: How Smart Companies Use Environmental Strategy to Innovate, Create Value, and Build Competitive Advantage.* New Haven, CT: Yale University Press, 2006.
Thomas L. Friedman	*Hot, Flat, and Crowded: Why We Need a Green Revolution and How It Can Renew America.* Release 2.0. New York: Farrar, Straus & Giroux, 2008.
Elizabeth Grossman	*High Tech Trash: Digital Devices, Hidden Toxics, and Human Health.* Washington, DC: Island, 2006.
R.E. Hester and R.M. Harrison, eds.	*Electronic Waste Management: Design, Analysis, and Application.* Cambridge, UK: Royal Society of Chemistry, 2009.

James Hoggan with Richard Littlemore	*Climate Cover-Up: The Crusade to Deny Global Warming.* Vancouver, BC: Greystone, 2009.
David Keith	*A Case for Climate Engineering.* Cambridge, MA: MIT Press, 2013.
Gerald Kutney	*Carbon Politics and the Failure of the Kyoto Protocol.* New York: Routledge, 2014.
Abrahm Lustgarten	*Hydrofracked? One Man's Mystery Leads to a Backlash Against Natural Gas Drilling.* New York: ProPublica, 2011.
Seamus McGraw	*The End of Country: Dispatches from the Frack Zone.* New York: Random House, 2011.
Jeffrey K. McKee	*Sparing Nature: The Conflict Between Human Population Growth and Earth's Biodiversity.* Piscataway, NJ: Rutgers University Press, 2003.
Tara Meixsell	*Collateral Damage: A Chronicle of Lives Devastated by Gas and Oil Development and the Valiant Grassroots Fight to Effect Political and Legislative Change.* Seattle: CreateSpace, 2010.
William Nordhaus	*The Climate Casino: Risk, Uncertainty, and Economics for a Warming World.* New Haven, CT: Yale University Press, 2013.

Naomi Oreskes and Erik M. Conway	*Merchants of Doubt: How a Handful of Scientists Obscured the Truth on Issues from Tobacco Smoke to Global Warming.* New York: Bloomsbury, 2010.
Garth W. Paltridge	*The Climate Caper: Facts and Fallacies of Global Warming.* London: Quartet Books, 2010.
Orrin H. Pilkey and Keith C. Pilkey	*Global Climate Change: A Primer.* Durham, NC: Duke University Press, 2011.
Eric Pooley	*The Climate War: True Believers, Power Brokers, and the Fight to Save the Earth.* New York: Hyperion, 2010.
Jermaine L. Price and Richard C. Cooper, eds.	*Electronic Waste: Reuse, Recycling, and Export Considerations.* Hauppauge, NY: Nova Science, 2012.
Alex Prud'homme	*The Ripple Effect: The Fate of Fresh Water in the Twenty-First Century.* New York: Scribner, 2011.
Maria Ronay	*We Have to Change: Taking Action to Stabilize Climate Change, Curb Population Growth Including Immigration, End Poverty, and the Liquidation of Nature's Capital.* Bloomington, IN: iUniverse, 2010.
Anand M. Saxena	*The Vegetarian Imperative.* Baltimore: Johns Hopkins University Press, 2011.

Jeremy Shere   *Renewable: The World-Changing Power of Alternative Energy.* New York: St. Martin's, 2013.

Giles Slade   *American Exodus: Climate Change and the Coming Flight for Survival.* Gabriola Island, BC: New Society, 2013.

Brian Sussman   *Climategate: A Veteran Meteorologist Exposes the Global Warming Scam.* Washington, DC: WND Books, 2010.

Alan Weisman   *Countdown: Our Last, Best Hope for a Future on Earth?* New York: Little, Brown, 2013.

Tom Wilber   *Under the Surface: Fracking, Fortunes, and the Fate of the Marcellus Shale.* Ithaca, NY: Cornell University Press, 2012.

Index

Department of Energy and Climate Change (Great Britain), 81, 85
Desalination of water, 38, 44, 73
Desertification, 148
Dimethyl sulfide (DMS) emissions, oceanic, 110
Distillation-powered fission, 73
Droughts, 22, 24, 93–94, 122
Dust bowls, 22

E

Earth
  absence of water supply dangers, 41–45
  cubic miles of water data, 43
  deforestation, 23–24, 23–25, 58, 61, 148–149
  global carbon pollution data, 95
  hydrologic cycle, 122–123
  loss of biogenetic diversity, 22–23
  oceanic gyres, 166–167, 169–170, 184
  overreliance on fossil fuels, 24–26
  shale rock formations, 119
  surface warming measurement, 112
  view of, from space, 92–93
Earth Day celebrations, 30
Economic opportunities, with renewable energy, 54–55
Einstein, Albert, 30
Eisenhower, Dwight D., 66
Electrical/electronic equipment, 133
Electrically-powered fission, 73

Electricity
  battery storage capacity, 70
  economic development role, 54–55
  global access limitations, 55
  power sources, 31, 32
  renewable energy conversion process, 52–53
  US use, growth data, 65
Electronic stewards (e-stewards), 144
Electronic waste (e-waste)
  Basel Action Network report, 142
  causal loop, *136*
  effects and hazards, 138–139
  environmental/health hazards, 132–139
  EU recycling, 138, 190–191
  exaggeration of environmental, health hazards, 140–145
  export ban efforts, 142–143
  global scale of problem, 137–138
  high volume concerns, 135–136
  limited public awareness, 135
  main issues, 135, 137
  OECD definition, 134
  recycling hotspots, 138, 142, 143–144
  transboundary movement, 133–134
  UN Environment Program study, 141, 143
  US e-waste, 141
  waste stream growth, 133
Energy access opportunity, with renewable energy, 54, 55–56
Energy security opportunity, with renewable energy, 54

R

S

availability crisis, 35–36
conservation/efficiency, improvements, 38
desalination technology, 38, 44, 73
energy and food nexus, 39–40
environmentalists' closed thinking, 44–45
fracking consequences, 120–125
global consumption facts, 37
global freshwater need projection, 119
green policies/economic growth, 39–40
groundwater depletion, 26, 35–36
hydropower, 51, 56, 58–59, 64
irrigation, 26, 37, 38, 44
needs assessment, 37
nuclear power scarcity solution, 68
oceanic DMS emissions, 110
peak water alarmists, 43
pollution and toxicity, 26–27, 36
public-private partnerships, 38–39

rising sea levels, 93
supply dangers, 33–40
UN-Water report, 123
USGS hydrologic cycle description, 122–123
See also Freshwater; Underwater sources of drinking water
Water Currents (National Geographic), 34, 35
Water pumps, 59
Water-for-profit companies, 121–122
Weinberg, Alvin, 75
Whales, ear wax samples, 19
White, Angelique, 167, 178–179
Wildfires, 15, 22, 93
Williams, Arthur R., 67–76
Wilson, Stiv, 165–176
Wind power, 31, 32, 42, 51, 58–59, 63–65
Wood's Hole Oceanographic Institute, 179
Woody, Todd, 117

Y

Yukhananov, Anna, 163